# THE NEW SOUTH

ABRAHAM LINCOLN EDITION

∴

VOLUME 42
THE CHRONICLES
OF AMERICA SERIES
ALLEN JOHNSON
EDITOR

GERHARD R. LOMER
CHARLES W. JEFFERYS
ASSISTANT EDITORS

*WADE HAMPTON*

Photograph by Brady.

# THE NEW SOUTH

## A CHRONICLE OF SOCIAL
## AND INDUSTRIAL EVOLUTION
## BY HOLLAND THOMPSON

NEW HAVEN: YALE UNIVERSITY PRESS
TORONTO: GLASGOW, BROOK & CO.
LONDON: HUMPHREY MILFORD
OXFORD UNIVERSITY PRESS
1919

# CONTENTS

# ILLUSTRATIONS

# THE NEW SOUTH

.·.

## CHAPTER I

### THE BACKGROUND

THE South of today is not the South of 1860 or
even of 1865.   There is a New South, though not
perhaps in the sense usually understood, for no expression has been more often misused in super-
ficial discussion.   Men have written as if the phrase
indicated a new land and a new civilization, utterly
unlike anything that had existed before and involving a sharp break with the history and the traditions of the past.   Nothing could be more untrue.
Peoples do not in one generation or in two rid
themselves entirely of characteristics which have
been developing for centuries.

There is a New South, but it is a logical development from the Old South.   The civilization of the
South today has not been imposed from without

but has been an evolution from within, though influenced by the policy of the National Government. The Civil War changed the whole organization of Southern society, it is true, but it did not modify its essential attributes, to quote the ablest of the carpetbaggers, Albion W. Tourgée. Reconstruction strengthened existing prejudices and created new bitterness, but the attempt failed to make of South Carolina another Massachusetts. The people resisted stubbornly, desperately, and in the end successfully, every attempt to impose upon them alien institutions.

The story of Reconstruction has been told elsewhere. [1] A combination of two ideas — high-minded altruism and a vindictive desire to humiliate a proud people for partisan advantage — wrought mischief which has not been repaired in nearly half a century. It is to be doubted, however, whether Reconstruction actually changed in any essential point the beliefs of the South. Left to itself, the South would not, after the War, have given the vote to the negro. When left to itself still later, it took the ballot away. The South would not normally have accepted the negro as a

---

[1] See *The Sequel of Appomattox*, by Walter Lynwood Fleming (in *The Chronicles of America*).

social equal. The attempt to force the barrier between the races by legislation with the aid of bayonets failed. Without the taste of power during the Reconstruction period, the black South would not have demanded so much and the determination of the white South to dominate would not perhaps have been expressed so bitterly; but in any case the white South would have dominated.

Economic and industrial development was hindered by Reconstruction. Men of vision had seen before the War that the South must become more nearly self-sufficient; and the results of the conflict had emphasized this idea. The South believed, and believes yet, that it was defeated by the blockade and not by military force. According to this theory, the North won because the South could not manufacture goods for its needs, because it did not possess ships to bring in goods from abroad, and because it could not build a navy to defend its ports. Today it is clear that the South never had a chance to win, so long as the will to conquer was firm in the North. As soon as the War was over, the demand for greater industrial development made itself felt and gained in strength when Reconstruction came; but during that period the people had to devote all their energies to living day by day, hoping for strength to endure. When property was being confiscated under the forms of law, only to be squandered by irresponsible legislators, there was little incentive to remake the industrial system, and the ventures of the Reconstruction government into industrial affairs were not encouraging. Farm property in the South — and little was left except farm property after the War — depreciated in value enormously in the decade following 1860. Grimly, sullenly, the white man of the South fought again to secure domination, this time, however, of his own section only and not of the nation. When this had been achieved, a large portion of the population was overcome by that deadly apathy so often remarked by travelers who ventured to visit the land as they would have visited Africa. The white South wished only to be let alone.

During this apathetic period there was some talk of the natural resources of the South; but there was little attempt on the part of Southerners to utilize these resources. There was talk of interesting foreign capital, but little effective work was done to secure such capital. Many men feared the new problems which such development might bring in its train, while others, more numerous, were merely indifferent or lukewarm. Many of those who vaguely wished for a change did not know how to set about realizing their desires. The few men who really worked to stimulate a quicker economic life about 1880 had a thankless and apparently a hopeless task.

Yet one must be careful not to write of the South as if it were a single country, inhabited by a homogeneous people. Historians and publicists have spoken, and continue to speak, of "Southern opinion" and of the "Southern attitude" as if these could be definitely weighed and measured. No one who really knows the whole South could be guilty of such a mistake. The first difficulty is to determine the limits of the South. The census classification of States is open to objection. Delaware, Maryland, and West Virginia are included in the South, and so is Kentucky. Missouri is excluded, but a place is made for the new State of Oklahoma. As to Delaware and Maryland, there may be a difference of opinion, though it is difficult to justify the inclusion of the former. West Virginia is certainly not Southern, socially, politically, or economically. Kentucky is doubtful, and it is difficult to see why Missouri should be excluded from any list which includes Kentucky. Oklahoma is difficult to classify. But, at any rate the South is a large country, with a great variety of soil, climate, and population. As the crow flies, the distance from Richmond to Memphis, in an adjoining State, is greater than from Richmond to Bangor, Maine. From Richmond to Galveston is farther than from Richmond to Omaha or Duluth. Atlanta is usually considered to be far down in the South, and yet the distance from Atlanta to Boston or Minneapolis is less than to El Paso. Again, New Orleans is nearer to Cincinnati than to Raleigh.

There were, moreover, many racial strains in the South. The Scotch-Irish of the Piedmont in the Carolinas had, and have yet, little in common with the French of Louisiana. The lowlander of South Carolina and the hill men of Arkansas differed in more than economic condition. Even in the same State, different sections were not in entire accord. In Virginia and the Carolinas, for example, economic conditions and traditions — and traditions are yet a power in the South — differed greatly in different sections.

As the years passed, apathy began to disappear in some parts of the South. Wiser men recognized that the old had gone never to return. Men began to face the inevitable. Instead of brooding upon

their grievances, they adjusted themselves, more
or less successfully, to the new economic and social
order, and by acting in harmony with it found that
progress was not so impossible as they had supposed. White planters found that the net returns
from their farms on which they themselves had
labored were greater than when a larger force of negroes had been employed; shrewd men began to put
their scanty savings together to take advantage of
convenient water power. Securing the bare necessities of life was no longer a difficult problem for
every one. Men began to find pleasure in activity
rather than in mere passivity or obstruction.

Somehow, somewhere, sometime, a new hopefulness was born and this new spirit — evidence of
new life — became embodied in "the New South."
The expression is said to have been used first by
General Adam Badeau when stationed in South
Carolina, but the New South of which he spoke was
not the New South as it is understood today. Many
others have used the term loosely to signify any
change in economic or social conditions which they
had discovered. The first man to use the expression in a way which sent it vibrating through the
whole nation was Henry W. Grady, the gifted editor of the *Atlanta Constitution*. In a speech made

in 1886 by invitation of the New England Society of New York City, he took for his theme "the New South" and delivered an oration which, judged by its effects, had some of the marks of greatness. "The South," he said, "has nothing for which to apologize. She believes that the late struggle between the States was war and not rebellion, revolution and not conspiracy." He went on, however, to express the feeling that the outcome had been for the best, and painted a picture of the new spirit of the South, a trifle enthusiastic perhaps, but still recognizable.

Today a New South may be said to be everywhere apparent. The Old South still exists in nooks and corners of many States, it is true: there are communities, counties, groups of counties, which cling to the old ideas. In the hearts of thousands of men and women the Old South is enshrined, and there is no room for the new; but the South as a whole is a New South, marked by a spirit of hopefulness, a belief in the future, and a desire to take a fuller part in the life of the nation. To trace the development of the new spirit and to discuss its manifestations is the purpose of this book.

# CHAPTER II

As the year 1877 was beginning, the carpetbag governments in nine of the Southern States had been already overthrown. In two other States were two sets of officers, one of which represented the great mass of the whites while the other was based upon negro suffrage and was supported by Federal bayonets. Both sides seemed determined, and trouble was expected. The Republican contestants in Florida had already yielded to a decision of the Supreme Court of the State, but in South Carolina and Louisiana the Republican claimants held on until the orders to withdraw the troops were given in April, 1877. The withdrawal of the troops marked the definite end of Reconstruction. The Democratic claimants then took undisputed possession of the executive and legislative departments of these States. The native whites were again in entire charge of all the States

9

which had seceded. They now had the task of rebuilding the commonwealths shattered by war and by the aftermath of war. A new era for the South had dawned, and here properly begins the history of the New South.

The first and most important problem, as the white South saw it, was the maintenance of white supremacy which had been gained with so much difficulty. In only three States — South Carolina, Mississippi, and Louisiana — were there negro majorities. Obviously, if the whites could be induced or coerced to stand together, they could continue to control the governments in eight of the seceding States. The negro population, however, was not distributed uniformly over any of these States, so that, no matter how great the white preponderance in the State as a whole, there were counties or other civil divisions where negroes were in the majority. This meant that the issue of white supremacy was present in every State, for the negro majorities in such counties could elect the local officers and control the local governments.

To attain a political consolidation of the white population all other issues must be subordinated. Differences of opinion and judgment must be held in abeyance. No question upon which white men might seriously disagree must be placed in the party platform, if any way to avoid such insertion could be found. If by any chance the majority adopted a course obnoxious to the minority, the decision must be accepted loyally if not cheerfully, and the full white vote must be cast. Objection to a candidate or measure must not be expressed at the ballot box. Personal ambition must be restrained, and weakness and even unfitness in a candidate must be overlooked for the sake of white solidarity.

The task of creating a permanently solid South was not easy. The Southerner had always been an individualist, freely exercising his right to vote independently, engaging in sharp political contests before 1861, and even during the War. The Confederate Congress wrangled impotently while Grant was thundering at the gates of Richmond. So strong was the memory of past differences, that old party designations were avoided. The political organization to which allegiance was demanded was generally called the Conservative party, and the Republican party was universally called the Radical party. The term Conservative was adopted partly as a contrast, partly because the peace party had been so called during the War, and especially because the name Democrat was obnoxious to so many old Whigs.    It was not until 1906 that the term Conservative was officially dropped from the title of the dominant party in Alabama.

It is not surprising that men continued to turn for leadership to those who had led in battle and, to a less extent, to those who had taken part in the civil government of the Confederacy.    But for the humiliations of Reconstruction, some of these men might have been discredited, but the bitter experiences of those years had restored them to popular favor.    As the Federal soldier marched out of the public buildings everywhere, the Confederate soldier marched in.    These men had led in the contest against the scalawags and the carpetbaggers and many had suffered thereby.    Now they came into their own.    In some States the organization of voters was almost military.

During the first years after the downfall of the Reconstruction governments the task of consolidating the white South was measurably achieved.    As some one flippantly put the case, there came to be in many sections "two kinds of people — Democrats and negroes."    It was the general feeling on the part of the whites that to fail to vote was shameful, to scratch a ticket was a crime, and to attempt to organize the negroes was treason to one's race. The "Confederate brigadier" sounded the rallying cry at every election, and a military record came to be almost a requisite for political preferment. Men's eyes were turned to the past, and on every stump were recounted again and again the horrors of Reconstruction and the valiant deeds of the Confederate soldiers.   What a candidate had done in the past in another field seemed more important even than his actual qualifications for the office to which he aspired.   A study of the *Congressional Record* or of lists of state officers proves the truth of this statement.   In 1882, fourteen of the twenty-two United States Senators from the seceding States had military records and three had been civil officers of the Confederacy.   Several States had solid delegations of ex-Confederate soldiers in both houses.   When one reads the proceedings of Congress, he finds the names of Vance and Ransom, Hampton and Butler, Gordon and Wheeler, Harris and Bate, Cockrell and Vest, Walthall and Colquitt, Morgan and Gibson, and dozens of other Confederate officers.

The process of unifying the white South was not universally successful, however.   Here and there were Republican islands in a Democratic or

Conservative sea. The largest and most important exception was the Appalachian South, divided among eight different States. It is a large region, to this day thinly populated and lacking in means of communication with the outside world. Though it has some bustling cities, thriving towns, and prosperous communities, the Appalachian South today is predominantly rural. In the 216 counties in this region or its foothills, there were in 1910 only 43 towns with more than 2500 inhabitants.

This Appalachian region had been settled by emigrants from the lowlands. Some of them were of the thriftless sort who were forced from the better lands in the East by the inexorable working of economic law. By far the greater part, however, were of the same stock as the restless pioneers who poured over the mountains to flood the Mississippi Valley. Students of the mountain people maintain that so small an accident as the breaking of a linchpin fixed one family forever in a mountain cove, while relatives went on to become the builders of new States in the interior. Cut off from the world in these mountains, there have been preserved to this day many of the idioms, folk-songs, superstitions, manners, customs, and habits of mind of Stuart England, as they were brought over by the early colonists. The steep farms afforded a scanty living, and though the cattle found luscious pasturage during the summer, they were half starved during the winter. If by chance the mountaineers had a surplus of any product, there was no one to whom they might sell it. They lived almost without the convenience of coinage as a means of exchange. Naturally in such a society there was no place for slaves, and to this day negroes are not welcome in many mountain counties. But though these mountain people have missed contact with the outside world and have been deprived of the stimulus of new ideas, they seldom give evidence of anything that can fairly be classed as degeneracy. Ignorance, illiteracy, and suspended or arrested development the traveler of today will find among them, and actions which will shock his present-day standards; but these same actions would hardly have shocked his own father's great-grandfather. These isolated mountaineers have been aptly called "our contemporary ancestors."

The same people, it is true, had poured out of their cabins to meet Ferguson at King's Mountain; they had followed Jackson to New Orleans and to Florida and they had felt the influence of the wave of nationalism which swept the country after the War of 1812. But back to their mountains they had gone, and the great current of national progress swept by them. The movement toward sectionalism, which developed after the Missouri Compromise, had left them cold. So the mountaineers held to the Union. They did not volunteer freely for the Confederacy, and they resisted conscription. How many were enlisted in the Union armies it is difficult to discover, certainly over 100,000. It is not surprising, therefore, that these people became Republicans and have so continued in their allegiance.

Another element in the population having great influence in the South — in North Carolina, at least — was the Society of Friends. It was strong in both the central and the eastern sections. Many, but by no means all, of the Quakers opposed the Civil War and, after peace came, opposed the men who had been prominent in the War, that is, the dominant party. In spite of the social stigma attaching to Republicanism, many of the Quakers have persisted in their membership in that party to the present day. In all the seceding States there was a Union element in 1861, and, while most of the men composing it finally went into the War with zeal, there were individuals who resisted stoutly.

During the War they were abused without stint, but this criticism had only the effect of making them more stubborn. They naturally became Republicans after the War and furnished some of the votes which made Reconstruction possible. With these may be classed the few Northern men who remained in the South after the downfall of the Reconstruction governments.

There was another class of people in the South, some of whom had been rabid secessionists and whose Republicanism had no other foundation than a desire for the loaves and fishes. The salaries attached to some of the Federal offices seemed enormous at that time and, before the prohibition wave swept the South, there were in the revenue service thousands of minor appointments for the faithful. These deputy marshals, "storekeepers and gaugers," and petty postmasters attempted to keep up a local organization. The collectors of internal revenue, United States marshals, other officers of the Federal courts, and the postmasters in the larger towns controlled these men and therefore the state organizations. These Federal officials broke the unanimity of the white South, and they were supported by thousands of negroes. Some individuals among them were shrewd politicians,

2

but the contest was unequal from the beginning. On one side was intelligence, backed by loyal followers fiercely determined to rule. On the other was a leadership on the whole less intelligent, certainly more selfish, with followers who were ignorant and susceptible to cajolery or intimidation.

Before the downfall of the Reconstruction governments, and in the first few years afterward, there was much intimidation of negroes who wished to vote. Threats of loss of employment, eviction from house or plantation, or refusal of credit were frequent. In many sections such measures were enough, and Democrats were ordinarily chosen at the polls. Where the negroes were in a larger majority, stronger measures were adopted. Around election time armed bands of whites would sometimes patrol the roads wearing some special badge or garment. Men would gallop past the houses of negroes at night, firing guns or pistols into the air and occasionally into the roofs of the houses. Negroes talking politics were occasionally visited and warned — sometimes with physical violence — to keep silent. On election day determined men with rifles or shotguns, ostensibly intending to go hunting after they had voted, gathered around the polls. An occasional random shot might kick up the dust near an approaching negro. Men actually or apparently the worse for liquor might stagger around, seeking an excuse for a fight. It is not surprising that among the negroes the impression that it was unwise to attempt to vote gained ground.

Less crude but no less effective methods were employed later. As candidates or party organizations furnished the ballots, the "tissue ballot" came into use. Half a dozen of these might easily be dropped into the box at one time. If the surplus ballots were withdrawn by a blindfolded official, the difference in length or in the texture or quality of the ballot made possible the withdrawal of an undue proportion of Republican votes. Usually separate boxes were supplied for different sets of officers, and it was often provided that a ballot in the wrong box was void. An occasional intentional shifting of boxes thus caused many illiterate negroes to throw away their votes. This scheme reached its climax in the "eight box law" of South Carolina which made illiterate voting ineffective without aid. Immediately after any literate Republican, white or black, left the polling place the boxes were shifted, and the illiterates whose tickets he had carefully arranged deposited their ballots in the wrong boxes. White boys of eighteen, if well grown, sometimes voted, while a young negro unable to produce any evidence of his age had difficulty in proving the attainment of his majority. In some precincts illiterate Republicans were appointed officers of elections, and then the vote was juggled shamelessly. A study of election returns of some counties of the black belt shows occasional Democratic majorities greater than the total white population. The same tricks which were so long practiced in New York and Philadelphia were successful in the South.

Conditions such as these were not prevalent over the entire South. In a large proportion of the voting precincts elections were as fair as anywhere in the United States; but it may be safely said that in few counties where the negroes approached or exceeded fifty per cent of the total population were elections conducted with anything more than a semblance of fairness. Yet in some sections the odds were too great, or else the whites lacked the resolution to carry out such extensive informal disfranchisement. For years North and South Carolina each sent at least one negro member to the House of Representatives and, but for flagrant gerrymandering, might have sent more. Indeed negro prosecuting attorneys were not unknown, and many of the black counties had negro officers. Some States, such as North Carolina, gave up local self-government almost entirely. The Legislature appointed the justices of the peace in every county, and these elected both the commissioners who controlled the finances of the county and also the board of education which appointed the school committeemen. Judges were elected by the State as a whole and held courts in all the counties in turn. To this day, a Superior Court judge sits only six months in one district and then moves on to another. Other States gave up local government to a greater or less extent, while still others sought to lessen the negro vote by strict registration laws and by the imposition of poll taxes.

In many sections the negro ceased to make any attempt to vote, and the Republican organization became a skeleton, if indeed it continued at all. There was always the possibility of a revival, however, and after 1876 the North often threatened Federal control of elections. The possibility of negro rule was therefore only suspended and not destroyed; it might at any time be restored by force. The possibility of the negro's holding the balance of power seemed dangerous and ultimately led to attempts to disfranchise him by law, which will be considered in another chapter.

The relation of the races was not the only question which confronted the whites when they regained control of the state governments. The problem of finance was equally fundamental. The increase in the total debt of the seceding States had been enormous. The difference between the debts of these States (excluding Texas) in 1860 and in the year in which they became most involved was nearly $135,000,000.[1] In proportion to the total wealth of these States, this debt was extremely high.

Not all of this increase was due to carpetbag government. While, of course, the debts incurred for military purposes had been repudiated in accordance with the Fourteenth Amendment, several of the States had issued bonds for other purposes during the War or immediately afterwards before the advent of the Reconstruction governments. There were other millions of unpaid interest on all varieties of debts incurred before or after 1860. The Reconstruction debts had been incurred for various purposes, but bonds issued ostensibly to aid

[1] See W. A. Scott, *The Repudiation of State Debts*, p. 276. Texas had practically no debt when it passed under Reconstruction government, but added $4,500,000 in the period. The total increase in the debt of all these Southern States was then nearly $140,000,000.

in building railroads, canals, or levees made up the greater part of the total. These bonds, however, had been sold at a large discount, and only a small part of the money realized was applied to actual construction.

Some of the States had escaped almost entirely any considerable increase of debt; others were burdened far beyond their ability to pay, especially as property valuations had declined nearly one-half.[1]

The wholesale repudiation of their debts injured the credit of all the Southern States, and they have been loudly denounced for their action. Their spokesmen have justified their procedure in regard to the bonds issued by the carpetbag legislatures on the ground that they were voted by venal governments imposed by military force; that many of the bonds were fraudulent on their face; and that those who purchased them at a great discount were simply gambling upon the chance that the governments issuing them would endure; that the greater part of these bonds were stolen by the officers; and that little or no benefit came to the State. Not all of the bonds which were repudiated or scaled down, however, belonged to this class. Many were undoubtedly valid obligations on the part of the

[1] See page 227 ff.

States. The repudiation of these bonds was excused on the ground that they were generally issued to aid railroads which had been practically seized by the Confederate or the United States governments and had been worn out for their benefit; that interest could not be paid during the war; and that war and the Reconstruction Acts had so reduced property values that payment of the full amount was impossible. The last reason is true of some States, though not of all. The prompt payment of interest on the reduced indebtedness has done much to restore the credit of the South, and the bonds of some States now sell above par.

Extravagance had helped to overthrow the carpetbag régime. The new governments were necessarily forced to be economical. Expenditures of all kinds were lessened. Government was reduced to its lowest terms, and the salaries of state officers were fixed at ridiculously small figures. Inadequate school taxes were levied; the asylums for the insane, though kept alive, could not take care of all who should have been admitted; appropriations for higher education, if made at all, were small; there was little or no social legislation. The politicians taught the people that low taxes were the greatest possible good and, when prosperity began to return and a heavier burden of taxation might easily have been borne, the belief that the efficiency of a government was measured by its parsimony had become a fixed idea.  There was little scandal anywhere.  No governments in American history have been conducted with more economy and more fidelity than the governments of the Southern States during the first years after the Reconstruction period.  A few treasurers defaulted, but in most cases their difficulties rose from financial incompetence rather than from dishonesty, for a good soldier did not necessarily make a good treasurer. Few fortunes were founded on state contracts. The public buildings erected were honestly built and were often completed within the limits of the original appropriations.  So small an amount was allowed that there would have been little to steal, even had the inclination been present.

The decline in the prices of agricultural products after 1875 made living harder.  The Greenback agitation [1] found some followers, and in a few scattered rural districts Greenbackers or Greenback Democrats were nominated.  In a few districts the white men ventured to run two tickets, and in a

[1] See *The Agrarian Crusade*, by Solon J. Buck (in *The Chronicles of America*).

few cases the Greenback candidate won. This activity was a precursor of the agrarian revolt which later divided the South. There were also some Republican tickets with qualifying words intended to catch votes, but they had little success.

Some strong men were sent to Congress, a very large proportion of whom had seen service in the Confederate army. Their presence aroused many sneers at "rebel brigadiers" and an immense amount of "bloody shirt" oratory. They accomplished little for their section or for the nation, as they were always on the defensive and could hardly have been expected to have any consuming love for the Union, in which they had been kept by force. They were frequently taunted in debate in the hope that indiscreet answers would furnish campaign material for use in the North. Sometimes they failed to control their tempers and their tongues and played into the hands of their opponents. They advocated no great reforms and showed little political vision. They clung to the time-honored doctrines of the Democratic party — tariff for revenue only, opposition to sumptuary laws, economy in expenditures, and abolition of the internal revenue taxes — and they made ponderous speeches upon the Constitution, "viewing with alarm" the encroachments of the Federal Government upon the sphere of action marked out for the States.

Partly because of constitutional objections, partly because of fear of Federal supervision of the administration of the measure, a majority of the Southern representatives opposed the Blair Bill, which might have hastened the progress of their section.   This measure, now almost forgotten, was much discussed between 1882 and 1890 when it was finally shelved.   It provided for national aid to education out of the surplus revenues of the Federal Government, the distribution to be made in proportion to illiteracy.   Though the South would have received a large share of this money, which it sorely needed for education, the experience of the South with Federal supervision had not been pleasant, and many feared that the measure might result in another Freedmen's Bureau.[1]   Not all Southerners, however, were opposed to the project. Dr. J. L. M. Curry, agent of the Peabody Fund, did valiant service for the bill, and some members of Congress were strong advocates of the measure.   Today we see a measure for national

[1] See *The Sequel of Appomattox*, by Walter Lynwood Fleming (in *The Chronicles of America*).

aid to education fathered by Southerners and almost unanimously supported by their colleagues.

Though rotation in office was the rule in the representation in the House, the policy of reëlecting Senators was generally followed, and some of them served long periods. Looking upon themselves as ambassadors of their States to an unfriendly court, they were always dignified and often austere. As time went on, their honesty, old-fashioned courtesy, and amiable social qualities gained for many the respect and affectionate esteem of their Northern colleagues. Many strong friendships sprang up, and through these personal relationships occasional bits of patronage and items of legislation were granted. Often, it is said, politicians who were accustomed to assail one another in public sought each other's society and were the best of friends in private. These Southern men were almost invariably a frugal lot who lived from necessity within their salaries and used no questionable means of increasing their incomes.

The election of Cleveland in 1884 gave to the South its first real participation in national affairs for a quarter of a century. Thomas F. Bayard of Delaware, L. Q. C. Lamar of Mississippi, and A. H. Garland of Arkansas were chosen for the

*L. Q. C. LAMAR*

From a photograph.

Gravure, Andersen-Lamb Co. N.Y.

Cabinet, from which the scholarly Lamar was transferred to the Supreme Court. John G. Carlisle of Kentucky was Speaker, and Roger Q. Mills of Texas became Chairman of the Ways and Means Committee of the House to succeed William R. Morrison. A fair share, if not more, of the more important diplomatic, consular, and administrative appointments went to Southerners. The South began to feel that it was again a part of the Union. However, though Cleveland had shown his friendliness to their section, the Southern politicians, usually intensely partisan, could not appreciate the President's attitude toward the civil service and other questions, and his bluntness offended many of them. They followed him on the tariff but opposed him on most other questions, for his theory of Democracy and theirs diverged, and his kindly attitude was later repaid with ingratitude.

During the period in which the "rebel brigadiers" had controlled their States a new generation had arisen which began to make itself felt between 1885 and 1890. The Grange had tried to teach the farmers to think of themselves as a class, and the skilled workmen in a few occupations, in the border States particularly, had been organized. The Greenback craze had created a distrust of the capitalists of the East. The fear of negro domination was no longer so overmastering, and the natural ambition of the younger men began to show itself in factional contests. Younger men were coveting the places held by the old war-horses and were beginning to talk of cliques and rings. The Farmers' Alliance was spreading like wildfire, and its members were expounding doctrines which seemed rank treason to the elderly gentlemen whose influence had once been so potent. It is now clear that their fall from power was inevitable, though they refused to believe it possible.

# CHAPTER III

## THE REVOLT OF THE COMMON MAN

PRACTICALLY all the farmers in the South, like those of the West, were chronically in debt, and after 1870 the general tendency of the prices of agricultural products was downward. In spite of largely increased acreage — partly, to be sure, because of it — the total returns from the larger crops were hardly so great as had been received from a much smaller cultivated area. The Southern farmer began to feel helpless and hopeless. Though usually suspicious of every movement coming from the North, he turned readily to the organization of the Patrons of Husbandry, better known as the Grange. In fact, the hopeless apathy of the Southern farmer observed by Oliver Hudson Kelley, an agent of the Bureau of Agriculture, is said to have determined him to found the order. In spite of the turmoil of Reconstruction, the organization appeared in South Carolina and Mississippi in 1871. Tennessee,

Missouri, and Kentucky had already been invaded. During 1872 and 1873, the order spread rapidly in all the States which may be called Southern. The highest number reached was in the latter part of 1875 when more than 6400 local granges were reported in the States which had seceded; and in Kentucky, Maryland, Delaware, West Virginia, and Missouri there were nearly 4000 more. The total membership in the seceding States was more than 210,000 and including the border States, over 355,000. Since negroes were not admitted, the proportion of the total white agricultural population in the Grange was perhaps as high in the South as in any other part of the Union. In the years that followed, the order underwent the same disintegration in the South as elsewhere.

As a class the Southern Grangers did not take an active part in politics. The overshadowing question of the position of their States in the Union and the desire to preserve white supremacy prevented any great independent movement. In a few instances, men ran for Congress as Independents or as Greenbackers, and in some cases they were elected; but the Southern farmers were not yet ready to break away from the organization which had delivered them from negro rule. There

was not at that time in the South the same opposition to railroads that prevailed in the West.
The need of railroads was felt so keenly that the
practice of baiting them had not become popular.  Some railroad legislation was passed, largely
through Granger influence, but it was not yet radical.  Nevertheless the Granger movement was by
no means without permanent influence.  It helped
to develop class consciousness; it demonstrated that
the Western and the Southern farmer had some
interests in common; and it also implanted in
people's minds the idea that legislation of an economic character was desirable.  Heretofore the
Southern farmer, so far as he had thought at all
about the relation of the State to industry, had
been a believer in *laissez faire*.  Now he began to
consider whether legislation might not be the remedy for poverty.  Out of this serious attention to
the needs of the farmer other organizations were
to arise and to build upon the foundations laid by
the Grange.

About 1875 there appeared in Texas and other
States local organizations of farmers, known as
Farmers' Alliances, and in 1879 a Grand State Alliance was formed in Texas.  The purposes were
similar to those set forth by the Grange.  In

3

Arkansas appeared the Agricultural Wheel and the Brothers of Freedom, which were soon consolidated. The Farmers' Union of Louisiana and the Alliance of Texas were also united under the name of the National Farmers' Alliance and Coöperative Union of America. This was soon united with the Arkansas Wheel, which had crossed state lines.

A session of the National Alliance was held at St. Louis in 1889 with delegates present from every Southern State, except West Virginia, and from some of the Middle Western States. The National Assembly of the Knights of Labor was also held in St. Louis at this time, and a joint declaration of beliefs was put forth. This platform called for the issue of more paper money, abolition of national banks, free coinage of silver, legislation to prevent trusts and corners, tariff reform, government ownership of railroads, and restriction of public lands to actual settlers.

The next year, the annual convention of the Alliance was held at Ocala, Florida, and the Ocala platform was published. This meeting recommended the so-called sub-treasury plan by which the Federal Government was to construct warehouses for agricultural products. In these the farmer might deposit his non-perishable agricultural products, and receive 80 per cent of their market value in greenbacks. Surely the Southern farmer had shaken off much of his traditional conservatism in approving such a demand as this! The explanation is not far to seek.

The high price of cotton in the years immediately following the War was the economic salvation of the South. Whatever may have been the difficulties in its production, the returns repaid the outlay and more. The quantity was less than the world demanded. Not until 1870–71 did the production approach that of the crops before the War. Then, with the increase in production and general financial stringency came a sharp decrease in price. Between 1880 and 1890 the price was not much above the cost of production, and after 1890 the price fell still lower. When middling cotton brought less than seven cents a pound in New York, the small producer got little more than five cents for his bale or two. The price of wheat and corn was correspondingly low, if the farmer had a surplus to sell at harvest time. If he bought Western corn or flour in the spring on credit, the price he paid included shrinkage, storage, freight, and the exorbitant profit of the merchant. The low price received by the Western producer had been much increased before the cereals reached the Southern consumer. The Southern farmer was consequently becoming desperate and was threatening revolt against the established order.

While Southern delegates joined the Western Alliance in the organization of the People's party in 1891 and 1892, the majority of the members in the South chose an easier way of attaining their object: they entered the Democratic primaries and conventions and captured them. In State after State, men in sympathy with the farmers were chosen to office, often over old leaders who had been supposed to have life tenure of their positions. In some cases these leaders retained their offices, if not their influence, by subscribing to the demands of the Alliance. Perhaps some could do this without reservation; others, Senators particularly, justified themselves on the theory that a legislature had the right to speak for the State and instruct those chosen to represent it.

The feeling of the farmer that he was being oppressed threatened to develop into an obsession. His hatred of "money-power," "trusts," "corners," and the "hirelings of Wall Street" found expression in his opposition to the local lawyers and merchants, and, in fact, to the residents of the towns in general. The idea began to grow up that any one living in a town was necessarily an enemy to the farmer. The prevalent agricultural point of view came to be that only the farmer was a wealth producer, and that all others were parasites who sat in the shade while he worked in the sun and who lived upon the products of his labor. This bitterness the farmer extended to the old political leaders whom he had regarded with veneration in the past. These old Confederate soldiers, he believed, had allowed him to be robbed.

The state Democratic Convention of Georgia in 1890 pledged all candidates for office to support the demands of the Farmers' Alliance, including the sub-treasury "or some better system." Senator John B. Gordon, however, refused to pledge himself and was reëlected nevertheless. The leader of the Alliance was nominated and elected governor. In Alabama, Reuben F. Kolb, the Commissioner of Agriculture, almost obtained the Democratic nomination for governor. Two years later, he again entered the primary and, declaring that he had been cheated out of the nomination, ran independently as the candidate of the Jeffersonian Democracy. On the face of the returns, the regular candidate was elected, but Kolb pointed out the fact that the Democratic majorities came from the black counties, while the white counties had given a majority for him. Again in 1894 Kolb entered the race for governor and again declared that he had been counted out, as he had not only the Jeffersonian Democracy behind him but also the endorsement of the Republicans and the Populists.

Undoubtedly the controlling influence in Democratic councils in some of the Southern States had been exercised by a very small element in the population. A few men, almost a "Family Compact" either held the important offices themselves, or decided who should hold them, and fixed the party policy so far as it had a policy other than the maintenance of white supremacy. The governments were generally honest, economical, and cheap. The leaders, partly because they themselves believed in limiting the function of government and partly because they believed that the voters would oppose any extension, had prevented any constructive legislation. Events showed that they had misunderstood their people. When the revolt came, the farmer legislators showed themselves willing to vote money liberally for education and for other purposes which were once considered outside the sphere of government.

South Carolina furnished the most striking example of this revolt. In that State the families which had governed before the War continued the direction of affairs. By a rather unusual compromise, the large western population of the State had been balanced against the greater wealth of the east. Consequently there was overrepresentation of the east after the negro had been deprived of the ballot. It was charged — and with some show of truth — that a small group of men clustering around Charleston exercised an entirely disproportionate share of influence in party management. The farmers, with a growing class consciousness, began to resent this injustice and found a leader ready and anxious to direct them.

In March, 1890, the delegates of the Farmers' Association decided to secure the nomination for governor for Benjamin R. Tillman, who had devoted much of his time for four years to arousing the farmers. The contest for the nomination was begun in May and, after a bitter struggle, Tillman won easily in the convention in September. The "straight outs," dazed and humiliated, ran an independent candidate. Tillman and his followers accepted the challenge and the conflict took form as a struggle between mass and class. The farmers' leader, though not himself illiterate, obscure, or poor, raged up and down the State frankly and brutally preaching class war. He held up Charleston as a sink of iniquity, and he promised legislation to cleanse it. Perhaps a majority of the whites really believed his charges and put faith in his doctrines. If not, the fetish of party regularity drew the votes necessary to make up the deficiency. Tillman had been regularly nominated in a Democratic convention, and South Carolinians had been trained to vote the party ticket. He was elected by a large majority.

At the end of Tillman's first term two years later, he was again a candidate, and the convention which nominated him approved the Ocala platform. Since the party machinery was in control of the Tillmanites, the opposition adopted the name "Cleveland Democracy" and sought to undo the revolution. The result was never doubtful. Tillman was reëlected by an overwhelming majority, and on the expiration of his term was sent to the United States Senate, which he shocked by his passionate utterances as he had so often shocked his own State. The attitude of the educated and cultivated part of the population of South Carolina toward Tillman affords a parallel to that

*BENJAMIN R. TILLMAN*

At about the time of his election as Governor of South Carolina in 1890. Photograph by Schloss, New York.

BENJAMIN R. TILLMAN

At about the time of his election as Governor of South Carolina
in 1890. Photograph by Schloss, New York.

of Tory England toward Lloyd George twenty years later. The parallel may be extended further. Tillman, in time, modified some of his extreme opinions, won over many of his opponents, and gained the respect of his colleagues just as Lloyd George has done; and South Carolina grew to have pride in her sturdy fighter whose life ended just as his fourth term in the Senate was almost done.

The election of Tillman as Governor and then as Senator was a real revolution, for South Carolina had been long represented in the United States Senate by Wade Hampton and Matthew C. Butler, both distinguished soldiers and representatives of the old régime. Hampton, under whose leadership the carpetbag government had been overthrown, had been a popular idol. Both he and Butler had won the respect of their colleagues in the Senate and had reflected credit upon their State. But such services now availed nothing. Both they and others like them were swept out, to be replaced by the partisans of the new order.

Nothing was omitted by the reformers to humiliate what had been the ruling portion of the population. The liquor traffic was made a state monopoly by the dispensary system modeled on the

Gothenburg plan: no liquor was sold to be drunk on the premises, and the amount allowed a purchaser was limited. It was hoped the revenue thus received would permit a considerable reduction in the tax rate. These hopes, however, were not realized, and scandals concerning the purchasing agency kept the State in a turmoil for years. Other legislation was more successful. An agricultural and mechanical college for men was founded at the old home of John C. Calhoun at Clemson. A normal and industrial college for girls has also proved very successful. The appropriations to the state university were reduced on the ground that it was an aristocratic institution, but on the other hand funds for public schools were increased.

Not all the members of the Alliance remained in the Democratic party. Populist electors were nominated in every Southern State in 1892, except in Louisiana, where a combined Republican and Populist ticket was named. In no State did the new party secure a majority, but in Alabama, Georgia, North Carolina, Tennessee, and Texas, the Populist vote was large. In North Carolina, always inclined to independence, the combined Republican and Populist vote was larger than that cast for Democratic electors. It was obvious that

Democratic supremacy was imperiled, if the new party continued its amazing growth.

The politicians, Republican and Democratic, set out to win the insurgents. Some shrewd political manipulators, scenting future profit for themselves, had joined the new movement and were willing to trade. During 1893, 1894, and 1895 the Republicans were generally successful. In many States there was more or less coöperation in state and county tickets, in spite of the disfavor with which the Republican party had been regarded in the South. In North Carolina J. C. Pritchard, a regular Republican, was elected to the United States Senate, to fill the unexpired term of Senator Vance, but the Populist state chairman, Marion Butler, cool, calculating, and shrewd, took the full term to succeed Senator Ransom. The Democratic party had maintained control for twenty years, and it was held responsible for all the ills from which the farmer suffered. Then, too, some of the leaders of the new party felt that they would have greater opportunities for preferment by coöperating with a party in which the number of white voters was small.

The doctrine of free silver had been making converts among the Democrats, however, and early in

1896 it was clear that a majority of the Southern delegates to the national convention would favor a silver plank. The action of the convention in nominating Bryan and Sewall is told in another volume.[1] Bryan was also endorsed by the Populist convention, but that convention refused to endorse Sewall and nominated Thomas E. Watson for Vice-President. A majority of the Populist convention favored a strict party fight, but the managers were shrewd, and the occasion manifestly offered great opportunities for trading. In twenty-six States the electoral tickets were divided between Democrats and Populists. Among these States were Arkansas, Louisiana, Missouri, and North Carolina. But coöperation with Republicans on local legislative and state tickets often occurred. In North Carolina, a fusion legislature was elected, and a Republican was chosen governor by the aid of Populist votes, though one faction of the Populists nominated a separate ticket. The judicial and congressional nominations were divided. The apparent inconsistency of voting for Bryan for President and at the same time supporting Republicans who might be expected to oppose

[1] *The Agrarian Crusade*, by Solon J. Buck (in *The Chronicles of America*).

him in Congress was accepted without flinching. According to the bargain made two years before, when a Republican was sent to the United States Senate for an unexpired term by the aid of the Populist votes, Senator Pritchard was reëlected.

The experience of North Carolina with fusion government was a reminder of the Reconstruction days. The Republicans had dilated upon "local self-government" and the Populists had swallowed the bait. The Legislature changed the form of county government, by which the board of county commissioners had been named by the justices of the peace, and made the board elective. This turned over to the blacks counties in which several of the largest towns in the State were situated. Negro politicians were chosen to office, and lawlessness and violence followed. In Wilmington there was an uprising of the whites, who took possession of the city government by force. The Legislature was again Democratic in 1898 and began to prepare an amendment which should disfranchise a large proportion of the 125,000 negro voters of the State. There was coöperation between the Republican and Populist organizations again in 1900, but too many Populists had returned to their former allegiance. The restrictive amendment, of which more will be said presently, was carried by an overwhelming majority at the special election in the summer, and at the regular election in November the Democratic ticket was chosen by an overwhelming majority.

The fusion of 1896 and the rising prices of agricultural products killed the Populist party in the South, but the influence of the movement remains to this day. It has had some effect in lessening political intolerance, for those of the Populists who returned to the Democratic party came back without apology, while others have since classed themselves as Republicans. The Populist attitude toward public education was on the whole friendly, and more money has since been demanded and expended for public schools.

Perhaps the greatest effect of the Populist movement was the overthrow of the old political organizations. In some States a few men had ruled almost by common consent. They had exerted a great influence upon legislation — not by use of the vulgar arts of the lobbyists, but by the plea of party advantage or by the prophecy of party loss. They had given their States clean government and cheap government, but nothing more. A morbid fear of taxation, or rather of the effects of taxation upon the people, was their greatest sin. The agrarian movement took them unawares. They were unable to realize that between the South of 1890 and another, older South, there was a great gap. They could not interpret the half-coherent speech of the small farmer, who had come to feel that he had been wronged and struck out blindly at those whom he had previously trusted. New and unknown men appeared in Washington to take the place of men whose character, ability, and length of service had made them national figures. The governorship of the States went to men whose chief qualifications seemed to be prominence in the affairs of the Alliance or else bitter tongues.

Though the Populists, for the most part, returned to the Democratic party, and the suffrage amendments, which will be mentioned presently, made the possibility of Republican success extremely remote, the "old guard" has never regained its former position. In all the Southern States party control has been for years in the hands of the common man. The men he chooses to office are those who understand his psychology and can speak his language. Real primary elections were common in the South years before they were introduced elsewhere, and the man who is the choice of the majority in the Democratic primary wins.

Some of the men chosen to high office in the State and nation are men of ability and high character, who recall the best traditions of Southern statesmanship; others are parochial and mediocre; and some are blatant demagogues who bring discredit upon their State and their section and who cannot be restrained from "talking for Buncombe."

The election of a Democratic President in 1884 had stirred the smoldering distrust of the South on the part of the North. The well-known fact that the negro vote in the South did not have the influence its numbers warranted aroused the North to demand a Federal elections law, which was voiced by bills introduced by Senator Hoar of Massachusetts and by Henry Cabot Lodge, then a member of the House of Representatives. Lodge's bill, which was passed by the House in 1890, permitted Federal officials to supervise and control congressional elections. This so-called "Force Bill" was bitterly opposed by the Southerners and was finally defeated in the Senate by the aid of the votes of the silver Senators from the West, but the escape was so narrow that it set Southerners to finding another way of suppressing the negro vote than by force or fraud. Later the division of the white vote by the Populist party also endangered white supremacy in the South.

In this same year (1890) Mississippi framed a new constitution, which required as a prerequisite for voting a residence of two years in the State and one year in the district or town.  A poll tax of two dollars — to be increased to three at the discretion of the county commissioners — was levied on all able-bodied men between twenty-one and sixty. This tax, and all other taxes due for the two previous years, must be paid before the 1st of February of the election year.  All these provisions, though applying equally to all the population, greatly lessened the negro vote.  Negroes are notoriously migratory, and a large proportion never remain two years in the same place.  The poll tax could not be collected by legal process, and to pay the tax for two years, four dollars or more, eight months in advance of an election, seemed to the average negro to be rank extravagance.  Moreover, few politicians are reckless enough to arrange for the payment of poll taxes in exchange for the promised delivery of votes eight months away, when half the would-be voters might be in another county, or even in another State.  To clinch the matter, the constitution further provided that after 1892, in addition to the qualifications mentioned above, a person desiring to vote must be able to read any

4

section of the constitution, "or he shall be able to understand the same when read to him, or give a reasonable interpretation thereof." Even when fairly administered, this section operated to disfranchise more negroes than whites, for fewer can read and fewer can understand a legal instrument. But it is obvious that the opportunities for discrimination are great: a simple section can be read to an illiterate white, while a more difficult section, filled with technicalities, may be read to a negro applicant; and the phrase "a reasonable interpretation" may mean one thing in the case of a negro and quite another where a white man is concerned. It is perhaps not surprising that only 5123 Republican votes were reported in 1896, and hardly more, in 1912, were cast for Taft and Roosevelt together.

South Carolina followed the lead of Mississippi a little more frankly in 1895, by adopting suffrage amendments which provided for two years' residence in the State, one year in the county, and the payment of a poll tax six months before the election. Up to 1898 any person who could read any section of the constitution, or could understand and explain it when read by the registration officer, could have his name placed upon a permanent roll and could vote thereafter, provided he satisfied the other requirements already mentioned. After January 1, 1898, every one presenting himself for registration had to be able to read and write any section of the constitution, or else must have paid taxes the preceding year on property assessed at three hundred dollars or over. The list of disqualifying crimes is long, including those of which negroes are most commonly found guilty, such as larceny, false pretence, bigamy, adultery, wife-beating, and receiving stolen goods. To insure the complexion of the permanent roll, the registration was conducted in each county by a board of "three discreet persons" appointed by the Governor, by and with the advice and consent of the Senate.

It would seem that either of these constitutions would serve to reduce the negro vote sufficiently, while allowing practically all white men to vote. Large discretion, however, is lodged in the officers of election, and Democratic control in these matters is safe only so long as the white men stick together. Louisiana went a step further in 1898 and introduced the famous "grandfather clause" into her constitution. Other requirements were similar to those already mentioned. Two years' residence in the State, one year in the parish, and six months in the precinct were preliminary conditions; in addition the applicant must be able to read and write in English or his mother tongue, or he must be the owner of property assessed for three hundred dollars or more.

This general requirement of literacy or ownership of property was waived, however, in case of foreigners naturalized before January 1, 1898, who had lived in the State five years, and in the case of men who had voted in any State before 1867, or of sons or grandsons of such persons. These could be placed upon a permanent roll to be made up before September 1, 1898, and should have the right to vote upon complying with the residence and poll tax requirements. Practically all white persons of native stock either voted in some State in 1867 or were descended from some one who had so voted. Few negroes in any State, and none in the South, were voters in that year. It is obvious that suffrage was open to white but barred to negro illiterates. Apparently the only whites debarred under this clause were the illiterate and indigent sons of foreign-born fathers.

North Carolina adopted a new suffrage article in 1900 which is much simpler than those just described. It requires two years' residence in the State, one in the county, and the payment of poll tax before the 1st of May in the election year. A uniform educational qualification is laid down, but the "permanent roll" is also included. No "male person who was on January 1, 1867, or at any other time prior thereto, entitled to vote under the laws of any State in the United States, wherein he then resided, and no lineal descendant of any such person shall be denied the right to register and vote at any election in the State by reason of his failure to possess the educational qualifications herein prescribed: *Provided* he shall have registered in accordance with the terms of this section prior to December 1, 1908." In other words, any white illiterate thirteen years old or over when the amendment was adopted would not be deprived of his vote because of the lack of educational qualifications. No other State had given so long a time as this.

The "grandfather clause" here was shrewdly drawn. Free negroes voted in North Carolina until 1835, and under the terms of the clause any negro who could prove descent from a negro voter could not be debarred because of illiteracy. Negroes voted in a few States in 1867, and they or their descendants were exempt from the educational test. Of course the number of these was negligible, and the clause accomplished precisely what it was intended to do — that is, it disfranchised a large proportion of the negroes and yet allowed the whites to vote. The extension of the time of registration until 1908, eight years after the amendment was adopted and six after it went into effect, made the disfranchisement of any considerable number of whites impossible.

Alabama followed in 1901, combining the South Carolina and the Louisiana plans and including the usual residence and poll tax requirements, as well as the permanent roll. This was to be made up before December 20, 1902, and included soldiers of the United States, or of the State of Alabama in any war, soldiers of the Confederate States, their lawful descendants, and "men of good character who understood the duties and obligations of citizenship under a republican form of government." After the permanent roll has been made up, the applicant for registration must be able to read and write and must have worked the greater part of the twelve months next preceding, or he or his wife must own forty acres of land or real estate or personal property assessed at not less than three hundred dollars. A long list of disqualifying crimes was added, including wife-beating and conviction for vagrancy. As if this were not enough, after

1903 an applicant for registration might be required to state where he had lived during the preceding five years, the name or names by which known, and the names of his employers. Refusal to answer was made a bar to registration, and wilful misstatement was regarded as perjury.

Oklahoma adopted its disfranchising amendment in 1910, without valid reason so far as any one outside the State could see, as the proportion of negroes was very small. An attempt was made permanently to disfranchise the illiterate negro by the "grandfather clause," while allowing illiterate white voters to vote forever. Other States allowed a limited time in which to register on a permanent roll, after which all illiterates were to be disfranchised. Oklahoma sought to keep suffrage permanently open to illiterate whites, while closing it to illiterate negroes. This amendment was declared unconstitutional by the United States Supreme Court in June, 1915, on the ground that a State cannot reëstablish conditions existing before the ratification of the Fifteenth Amendment, even though the disfranchising amendment contained no "express words of exclusion" but "inherently brings that result into existence."[1] What the Court will

[1] Guinn vs. United States, 238 U. S., 347.

do with other similar constitutional amendments when they are brought before it is not so certain. All differ somewhat, and it is possible that the Court may let the whole or a part of some of them stand. If not, it is probable that straight educational and property qualifications will be substituted. In fact, if the Court disapproves the permanent roll but allows the remainder to stand, educational and property qualifications will prevail in several States.

All these plans for disfranchisement have accomplished the desired results up to the present time. The negro vote has been greatly reduced and elections are decided by the votes of white men. In some States, negroes who could easily pass the tests no longer take the trouble to go to the polls. The number of white voters also grows smaller. Some fail to pay the poll tax, and others stay away from the polls because, as a rule, the result has been decided in the primary elections. Since a Democratic nomination is practically equivalent to election, many voters who have taken part in the primaries neglect to vote on election day. Only in North Carolina is there evidence of the growth of a strong Republican opposition. In 1908, Taft received over 114,000 votes, and the Republican candidate for governor 107,000. In 1916 Hughes received 120,000 votes as against 168,000 for Wilson.

What was done with the negro when he was thus rendered politically helpless? Was there an attempt to take from him other things than the ballot? The answer must be in the affirmative. Men advocated segregation in common carriers, in public places, and even in places of residences. An attempt to confine appropriations for negro schools to the amount of taxes directly paid by the negroes has been made; men have sought office on a platform of practical serfdom for the negro. But although some few have achieved temporary successes — at least they have been elected — their programs have not been carried out. The "Jim Crow" car is common and the negro schools do not get appropriations equal to those of the whites, but little else has been done. In fact, evidences of a reaction in favor of the negro soon became apparent. The late Governor Charles B. Aycock of North Carolina at the beginning of this century won his triumphs on a platform of justice for the negro.

The question of the liquor traffic began to engage the attention of the Southern people very soon after the end of Reconstruction. The great problem was the sale of liquor in the unpoliced country districts, and especially to negroes. By special legislative acts forbidding the sale of liquor within a given number of miles of a church or a school a large part of the South was made dry. Local option acts continued the restrictive work until the sale of liquor outside of the larger incorporated towns became rare. In some States, acts applying to the whole State forbade the sale outside of towns. By concentrating their efforts upon the towns, the anti-saloon forces made a large number of them dry also, but there was so much illicit sale that employers often found that Monday was a wasted day.

State wide prohibition began in 1907 with Oklahoma and Georgia, and State after State followed until, in 1914, ten States were wholly dry, and in large areas of the other Southern States the sale of intoxicants was forbidden through local option. Southern members of Congress urged the submission of the Eighteenth Amendment to the Constitution, forbidding manufacture or sale of intoxicants in the nation. Every Southern State promptly ratified the Amendment when it was submitted by Congress.

Unfortunately many negroes when deprived of

alcohol began to use drugs, such as cocaine, and the effect morally and physically was worse than that of liquor. The "coke fiend" became a familiar sight in the police courts of Southern cities, and the underground traffic in the drug is still a serious problem. The new Federal law has helped to control the evil, but both cocaine and alcohol are still sold to negroes, sometimes by pedlars of their own race, sometimes by unscrupulous white men. The consumption of both is less, however, than before the restrictive legislation. The South has traveled far from its old opposition to sumptuary laws. Like State Rights, this principle is only invoked when convenient. Starting largely as a movement to keep whiskey from the negro and, to a somewhat less extent, from the white laborer, prohibition has become popular. On the whole it has worked well in the South though "moonshining" is undoubtedly increasing. The enormous price eagerly paid for whiskey in the "bone-dry" States has led to a revival of the illicit distillery, which had been almost stamped out.

# CHAPTER IV

## THE FARMER AND THE LAND

THE end of Reconstruction found the tenant system and the "crop lien" firmly fastened upon the South. The plantation system had broken down since the owner no longer had slaves to work his land, capital to pay wages, or credit on which to borrow the necessary funds. Many of the great plantations had already been broken up and sold, while others, divided into tracts of convenient size, had been rented to white or negro tenants. What had been one plantation became a dozen farms, a score, or even more. Men who owned smaller tracts found it difficult to hire or to keep labor, and many retained only the land which they or their sons could work and rented the remainder of their farms. This system is still characteristic of Southern agriculture.

Few of the landless whites and practically none of the negroes had sufficient money reserve to maintain themselves for a year and hence no capital to apply to the land on which they were tenants. Yet the land was there ready to produce, the labor was there, more or less willing to work if it could but live while the crop was growing. The country merchant had already assumed the office of banker to the tenant farmer, and this position he still holds in spite of all efforts to dislodge him. His customers include not only tenants but some land-owners, white or black. They buy from him, during the months before the crop is gathered, the food, clothing, and other supplies necessary for existence, and as many simple luxuries as he will permit. When the crops are gathered, he buys them, or at least the share of them belonging to the tenant, subtracts the store accounts, and turns over the surplus, if any, to the farmers.

Unlike other bankers, the merchant charges no interest upon the capital he advances, but he is paid nevertheless. For every pound of bacon, meal, and flour, for every gallon of molasses, for every yard of cloth, for every plug of tobacco or tin of snuff which the customer consumes during the spring and summer, an advanced price is charged to him on the merchant's books. With thousands of these merchants selling to hundreds of thousands of farmers over a wide area, it is of course impossible to state the average difference between credit and cash prices. Investigations made in different sections show a wide variation depending upon custom, competition, the reliability and industry of the customer, the amount of advances, and the length of credit. Since a large part of the advances are made during the six, or even four months before the crops are gathered, the difference between cash and credit prices amounts often to an interest charge of forty to one hundred per cent or even more a year. These advanced credit prices, and consequently the high interest rates, may be paid not only upon food, clothing, and other personal goods, but also, occasionally, upon tools, farming implements, fertilizers, and work animals.

The merchant is supposed to be protected against loss by the institution of the crop lien and the chattel mortgage. By one or the other of these the farmer is enabled to mortgage his growing, or even his unplanted crops, his farming implements, his cattle, and horses, if he owns them. If he is a land-owner, the land may be included in a mortgage as additional security. The crop is conveyed to the mortgagee as in an ordinary land mortgage, and the tenant cannot hold back his crop for a better price, or seek a better market for any part of it, until all his obligations have been settled. Disposing of mortgaged property is a serious offense and no one not desirous of abetting fraud will buy property which he has reason to suspect has been mortgaged. As a result of this system in some sections, years ago, nine-tenths of the farmers were in debt. Undoubtedly the prices credited for the crops have been less than might have been obtained in a market absolutely free. If the crops a farmer raises bring less than the advances, the balance is carried over to the next year and no other merchant will give credit to a man whose accounts with his former creditor are not clear. In the past the signing of one of these legal instruments has often reduced the farmer to a state of peonage.

Naturally the merchant who has begun to extend credit, sometimes before the seed is in the ground, has a voice in deciding what crops shall be planted. The favorite crops in the past have been tobacco and cotton, particularly the latter. Both contain comparatively large value in small bulk; both can be stored conveniently, with little danger of deterioration; neither is liable to a total failure; a ready market for both is always available; and neither tempts the thief until it is ripe. Only winter wheat, sown in the fall and reaped in early summer, is grown in the South, and the crop is somewhat uncertain. A tenant who has secured advances on a crop of wheat during the fall and winter may easily move to an adjoining county or State in the spring and plant cotton there. Half a crop of corn may easily be stolen, eaten by animals, or consumed by the tenant while still green. A further reason for not encouraging the production of corn and wheat is the profit the merchant makes by the sale of imported flour, meal, and bacon. Cotton is therefore almost the only product of sections admirably suited to the growing of corn or to the raising of hogs. The country merchant has helped to keep the South poor.

Yet in spite of the apparently exorbitant percentage of profit, few country merchants become rich. In a year of drouth, or of flood, many of their debtors may not be able to pay their accounts, even though their intentions are of the best. Others may prove shiftless and neglect their fields. Still others may be deliberately dishonest and, after getting as large advances as possible, abandon their crops leaving both the landowner and the merchant in the lurch. These creditors must then either attempt to harvest the crop by hired labor, with

## A FIELD OF TOBACCO

From a photograph taken near Lexington, Kentucky, in the famed Blue Grass Region. Copyright by Underwood and Underwood, New York.

A FIELD OF TOBACCO

From a photograph taken near Lexington, Kentucky, in the famed Blue Grass Region. Copyright by Underwood and Underwood, New York.

the hope of reducing their loss, or else charge the whole to profit and loss.   The illness or death of the debtor may also prevent the proper cultivation of the crop he has planted.   For these different reasons every country merchant is likely to accumulate many bad debts which may finally throw him into bankruptcy.   Those who succeed are exceptionally shrewd or very fortunate.

The relation of the tenant to his landlord varies in different parts of the South.   Many different plans of landholding have been tried since 1865, and traces of all of them may be found throughout the length and breadth of the South.   One was a modified serfdom, in which the tenant worked for the landlord four or five days in every week for a small wage.   In addition he had a house, firewood, and several acres of land which he might cultivate on his own account.   According to another plan, the landlord promised to pay a fixed sum of money to the laborer when the crop was gathered.   Both plans had their origin primarily in the landlord's poverty, but were reënforced by the tenant's unreliability.   These plans, as well as combinations of these with some others to be mentioned, have now practically died out.   There remain the following alternatives: land may be rented for a fixed sum of

5

money per acre, to be paid when the crops are sold, or for a fixed quantity of produce, so many bushels of corn or so many pounds of cotton being paid for every acre; or, more commonly, land may be rented on some form of share tenancy by which the risk as well as the profit is shared by both tenant and landowner.

Share tenancy assumes various forms. In some sections a rough understanding grew up that, in the division of a crop, one-third was to be allotted to the land, one-third to live stock, seed, and tools, and one-third to labor. If the tenant brought nothing but his bare hands, he received only the share supposed to be due to labor; if he owned working animals and implements, he received in addition the share supposed to be due to them. This arrangement, modified in individual cases, still persists, especially where the tenants are white. As various forms of industrial enterprise have continued to draw labor from the farms, the share assigned to labor by this form of tenancy has increased until, in perhaps the greater part of the South and certainly in the cotton-growing sections, it is usually one-half.

The ordinary arrangement of share tenancy under which the negro in the cotton belt now works provides that the landowner shall furnish a cabin in which the family may live and an acre or two for a garden.    In addition, working stock, implements, and seed are supplied by the owner of the land. Both tenant and owner share the cost of fertilizers if any are used, and divide equally the expenses of preparing the crop for market and the proceeds of the sale.    This arrangement means, of course, that the capitalist takes the laborer into a real partnership.    Both embark in a venture the deferred results of which are dependent chiefly upon the industry and good faith of the laborer.    By a seeming paradox it is only the laborer's unreliability which gives him such an opportunity, for if he were more dependable, the landowner would prefer in most cases to pay wages and take the whole of the crop.    Because the average negro laborer cannot be depended upon to be faithful, he is given a greater opportunity, contrary to all ordinary moral maxims.

When the share tenant lives on the land he may be a part of two different systems.    There are some large plantations over which the owners or managers exercise close supervision.    The horses or, more generally, the mules are housed in large common stables or sheds and are properly looked after.

Some attempt is made to see that tools and implements are kept in order. If the tenant falls behind in his work and allows his crop to be overrun with grass or is unable to pick the cotton as it opens, the owner hires help, if possible, and charges the cost against the tenant. In other words, the owner attempts to apply to agriculture some of the principles of industrial organization. The success of such attempts varies. The negro tenant generally resents close supervision; but on the other hand he enjoys the community life of a large plantation. In the end, in the majority of cases the personal equation determines whether the negro stays or moves.

At the other extreme is the landowner who turns over his land to the negro and hopes for some return. If the tenant is industrious and ambitious, the landowner gets something and is relieved of the trouble of supervision. Often, however, he finds at the end of the year that the mules have deteriorated from being worked through the day and driven or ridden over the country at night; the tools and implements are broken or damaged; and the fences have been used for firewood, though an abundant supply could have been obtained by a few hours' labor. Very often the landlord's share of the small crop will not really compensate him for the depreciated value of his property, for land rented without supervision is likely to decrease in fertility and to bring in meager returns.

A more successful arrangement between the two extremes is often seen in sections where the population is largely white and land is held in smaller tracts.   Here a white farmer who owns more land than he or his sons can cultivate marks off a tract for a tenant, white or black, who may be said to work with his landlord.   Both he and others of his family may work an occasional day for the landlord, receiving pay either in kind or in cash.   Relations between such families often become close, and the tenant may remain on the property for years. In some sections there are numerous examples of what might be called permanent tenants.   Sometimes such a tenant ultimately purchases the land upon which he has worked or other land in the neighborhood.

The plantation owner may be a merchant-landlord also and may furnish supplies to his tenants. He keeps only staple articles, but he may give an order on a neighboring store for those not in stock or may even furnish small sums of money on occasion.   The tenants are not allowed to buy as much as they choose either in the plantation store or in the local store at the crossroads. At the beginning of the year the landlord or the merchant generally allows a credit ranging from fifty to two hundred dollars but rarely higher and attempts to make the tenant distribute the purchases over the whole period during which the crop is growing. If permitted, many, perhaps a large majority of the tenants, might use up their credit months before the crop was gathered. In such cases the merchant or landlord, or both, must make further advances to save what they have already invested or else must see the tenant abandon his crops and move.

These relations between landlord and tenant show much diversity, but certain conditions prevail everywhere. Few tenants can sustain themselves until the crop is gathered, and a very large percentage of them must eat and wear their crops before they are gathered — a circumstance which will create no surprise unless the reader makes the common error of thinking of them as capitalists. Though the landlord in effect takes his tenants into partnership, they are really only laborers, and few laborers anywhere are six or eight months ahead of destitution. How many city laborers, even those with skilled trades, could exist without credit if their wages were paid only once a year? How many of them would have prudence or foresight enough to conserve their wages when finally paid and make them last until the next annual payment? The fault for which the tenant is to be blamed is that he does not take advantage of two courses of action open to him: first, to raise a considerable part of the food he consumes; and second, to struggle persistently to become independent of the merchant. Thousands of tenants have achieved their economic freedom, and all could if they would only make an intelligent and continued effort to do so.

Nowhere else in the United States has the negro the same opportunity to become self-sustaining, but his improvidence keeps him poor. Too often he allows what little garden he has to be choked with weeds through his shiftlessness. One of the shrewdest observers and fairest critics of the negro, Alfred Holt Stone, says of the Mississippi negro: "In a plantation experience of more than twelve years, during which I have been a close observer of the economic life of the plantation negro, I have not known one to anticipate the future by investing the earnings of one year in supplies for the next. . . . The idea seems to be that the money from a crop already gathered is theirs, to be spent as fancy suggests, while the crop to be made must take care of itself, or be taken care of by the 'white-folks.'"[1] This statement is not so true of the negroes of the Upper South, many of whom are more intelligent, and have developed foresight and self-reliance.

The theory that there is an organized conspiracy over the whole South to keep the negro in a state of peonage is frequently advanced by ignorant or disingenuous apologists for the negro, but this belief cannot be defended. The merchants usually prefer to sell for cash, and more and more of them are reluctant to sell on credit. In some cotton towns no merchant will sell on credit, and the landlord is obliged to furnish supplies to those who cannot pay. The landowners generally would much prefer a group of prosperous permanent tenants who could be depended upon to give some thought to the crop of the future as well as to that of the present. In the South as a whole the negro finds little difficulty in buying land, if he can make a moderate first payment. It is true that some are cheated by the merchant or the landlord. Prices charged for supplies are too high, and the prices credited for crops are too low, but the debtors are hardly swindled to

[1] Stone, *Studies in the American Race Problem*, p. 188.

a greater extent than the ignorant and illiterate elsewhere.

The condition of the white tenant is sometimes little better than that of the negro. He usually farms a larger tract, 83.8 acres on the average (in 1910), as against 39.6 acres for the negro, and he is on the whole more prosperous; but there are many who live from hand to mouth, move frequently, habitually get into debt to the merchant or the landlord, and have little or no surplus at settling time. In the South in 1910 there were 866,000 white tenant farmers who cultivated 20.5 per cent of all the land, and since that time white tenancy has been increasing. The increase of land owner-ship is greater among the negroes than among the whites, who are in many cases illiterates. This il-literacy is one cause of their poverty, but not the only cause: a part of it is moral, involving a lack of steadfast purpose, and a part is physical. The re-searches conducted by the United States Govern-ment, the state boards of health, and the Rocke-feller Foundation show clearly that much of the indolence charged to the less prosperous Southern rural whites is due to the effect of the hookworm, a tiny intestinal parasite common in most tropical and subtropical regions and probably brought from Africa or the West Indies by the negro. The Rockefeller Foundation is now spending nearly $300,000 a year in financing, wholly or in part, attempts to eradicate the disease in eight Southern States and in fifteen foreign countries.

The parasite enters the body from polluted soil, usually through the feet, as a large part of the rural population goes barefoot in the summer; it makes its way to the intestinal canal, where it fixes itself, grows, and lays eggs which are voided and hatch in the soil. Since most country districts are without sanitary closets, reinfection may occur again and again, until an individual harbors a host of these tiny bloodsuckers, which interfere with his digestion and sap his vitality. It is now believed that the morbid appetites of the "clay eaters" are due to this infection. The fact that the negro who introduced the curse is less susceptible to the infection and is less affected by it than the white man is one of life's ironies.

There is a brighter side to this picture, however. Of all the cultivated land in the South 65 per cent is worked by owners (white 60.6 per cent; colored 4.4 per cent) and this land is on the whole much better tilled than that let to tenants. It is true that some of the landowners are chronically in debt, burdened with mortgages and with advances for supplies. Some of them probably produce less to the acre than tenants working under close supervision, but the percentage of farms mortgaged is less in the South than in any other part of the country except the Mountain Division, and unofficial testimony indicates that few farms are lost through foreclosure.

For years the agricultural colleges and the experiment stations offered good advice to the Southern farmer, but they reached only a small proportion. Their bulletins had a small circulation and were so full of technical expressions as to be almost unintelligible to the average farmer. Recently the writers have attempted to make themselves more easily understood, and the usefulness of their publications has consequently increased. The bulletins of the Department of Agriculture are read in increasing numbers, and several agricultural papers have a wide circulation. The "farmer's institutes" where experts in various lines speak on their specialties are well attended, and the experimental farms to which few visitors came at first are now popular.

Two other agencies are doing much for agricultural betterment. One is the county demonstrator,

and the other boys' and girls' clubs. Both are
due to the foresight and wisdom of the late Dr.
Seaman A. Knapp, of the United States Department
of Agriculture. As early as 1903 Dr. Knapp had
been showing by practical demonstration how the
farmers of Texas might circumvent the boll weevil,
which was threatening to make an end of cotton-
growing in that State. He was able to increase
the yield of cotton on a pest-ridden farm. The
idea of the boys' corn club was not new when Dr.
Knapp took it up in 1908 and made it a national institution. The girls' canning club was soon
added to the list, and then came the pig club for
boys and the poultry club for girls.

The General Education Board, which, with its
large resources, had been seeking the best way to
aid education in the South, was forced to the conclusion that any educational development must be
preceded by economic improvement. The farm
production of the South was less than that of other
sections, and until this production could be increased, taxation, no matter how heavy, could not
provide sufficient money for really efficient schools.
After a study of the whole field of agricultural
education, the ideas of Dr. Knapp were adopted
as the basis of the work and, by arrangement with

the Department of Agriculture, Dr. Knapp himself was placed in charge. The appropriations to the Department of Agriculture had been made for the extermination or circumvention of the boll weevil and could not be used for purely educational work in States where the weevil had not appeared. A division of territory was now made: the Department financed demonstration work in those States affected by the pest and the General Education Board bore the expense in the other States. Entire supervision of the work was in the hands of the Department of Agriculture, which made all appointments and disbursed all funds. The Board furnished funds but assumed no authority. The history issued by the General Education Board says: "Dr. Knapp endeavored to teach his hearers not only how to raise cotton and corn, but how to conduct farming as a business — how to ascertain the cost of a crop, how to find out whether they were making or losing money. As rapidly as possible the scope was broadened for the purpose of making the farmer more and more independent. He was stimulated to raise stock, to produce feed and forage for his stock, and to interest himself in truck gardening, hog-raising, etc."

The method used was to appoint county, district,

and state demonstration agents who would in-
duce different farmers to cultivate a limited area
according to specific directions. As these agents
were appointed by the Department of Agriculture,
the farmer was flattered by being singled out by
the Government. In most cases the results of the
experiments were far superior to those which the
farmer had obtained merely by following tradition,
and he usually applied the successful methods to
his whole farm. Some of his neighbors, who visited
the demonstration plot to scoff at the idea that any
one in Washington could teach a farmer how to
grow cotton or corn, were wise enough to recognize
the improvement and to follow the directions.
Every successful demonstration farm was thus a
center of influence, and the work was continued
after Dr. Knapp's death under the charge of his
son, Bradford Knapp.

The idea of the boys' corn club was vitalized in
1908 by Dr. Knapp, who planned to establish a
corn club in every neighborhood, with county and
state organizations. Each boy was to cultivate a
measured acre of land in corn, according to directions and keep a strict account of the cost. The
work of his father, or of a hired man, in ploughing
the land must be charged against the plot at the

market rate. Manure, or fertilizer, and seed were likewise to be charged, but the main work of cultivation was to be done by the boy himself. The crop was to be measured by two disinterested witnesses who should certify to the result. Local pride was depended upon to furnish prizes for the county organization, but the most successful boys in every State were to be taken on a trip to Washington, there to shake hands with the Secretary of Agriculture and the President. This appeal to the imagination of youth was a master touch.

Thousands of boys were interested and achieved results which were truly startling. In every State the average yield from the boys' acres was larger than the state average, in some cases almost five times as great. One South Carolina boy produced on his acre in 1910 over 228 bushels, and in 1913 an Alabama boy reached high-water mark with nearly 233 bushels. Hundreds of boys produced over 100 bushels to the acre, and the average of the boys in South Carolina was nearly 69 bushels, compared with an average of less than 20 for the adult farmers. The pig clubs which followed have likewise been successful and have stimulated an interest in good stock and proper methods of caring for it. Many country banks have financed these operations by buying hogs by the carload and selling to the club members on easy terms.

Girls' canning clubs were organized by Dr. Knapp in 1910. Girls were encouraged to plant a tenth of an acre in tomatoes. Trained demonstrators then traveled from place to place and showed them how to use portable canning outfits. The girls met, first at one house and then at another, to preserve their tomatoes, and soon they began to preserve many other vegetables and fruits. Two girls in Tennessee are said to have preserved 126 different varieties of food. Some of these clubs have gained more than a local reputation for their products and have been able to sell their whole output to hotels or to institutions. Though the monetary gain has been worth something, the addition to the limited dietary of the homes has been worth more, and the social influence of these clubs has been considerable. The small farmer in the South is not a social being, and anything which makes for coöperation is valuable. The poultry clubs which were an extension of the canning club idea have been successful. The club idea, indeed, has been extended beyond the limits of the South. Congress, recognizing its value, has taken over and extended the work and has supported it liberally. Today market-garden clubs for the manufacturing cities, potato clubs, mother-and-daughter clubs, and perhaps others have grown out of the vision of Dr. Knapp.

Though these activities have had a great effect in improving the South, that section has not yet been transformed into an Eden. In spite of farm demonstrations, experiment stations, and boys' and girls' clubs, the stubborn inertia of a rural population fixed on the soil has only been shocked, not routed. Much land is barely scratched instead of being ploughed deep; millions of acres bear no cover crops but lose their fertility through the leaching of valuable constituents during the winter. Fertilizer is bought at exorbitant prices, while the richness of the barnyard goes to waste, and legumes are neglected; land is allowed to wash into gullies which soon become ravines. Farms which would produce excellent corn and hay are supplied with these products from the Middle West; millions of pounds of Western pork are consumed in regions where hogs can be easily and cheaply raised; butter from Illinois or Wisconsin is brought to sections admirably adapted to dairying; and apples from Oregon and honey from Ohio are sold in the towns. In several typical counties an average of $4,000,000 was sent abroad for products which could easily

6

have been raised at home. In Texas some of the bankers have been refusing credit to supply merchants who do not encourage the production of food crops as well as cotton.[1]

Throughout the South there are thousands of homes into which no newspaper comes, certainly no agricultural paper, and in which there are few books, except perhaps school books. The cooking is sometimes done with a few simple utensils over the open fire. Water must be brought from a spring at the foot of the hill, at an expenditure of strength and endurance. The cramped house has no conveniences to lighten labor or to awaken pride. The overworked wife and mother has no social life, except perhaps attendance at the services at the country church to which the family rides in a springless wagon. Such families see their neighbors prosper without attempting to discover the secret for themselves. Blank fatalism possesses them. They do not realize that they could prosper. New methods of cultivation, they think, are not for them since they have no capital to purchase machinery.

On the other hand, one sees more Ford cars than

[1] An illuminating series of studies of rural life is being issued by the Bureau of Extension of the University of North Carolina.

teams at many country churches, and many larger automobiles as well.  Some Southern States are spending millions for better roads, and the farmer or his son or daughter can easily run into town in the afternoon carrying a little produce which more than pays for any purchases.  Tractors are seen at work here and there, and agricultural machinery is under the sheds.  Many houses have private water systems and a few farmers have harnessed the brooks for electric lights.  The gas engine which pumps the water runs the corn sheller or the wood saw.  The rural telephone spreads like a web over the countryside.  Into these houses the carrier brings the daily or semi-weekly paper from the neighboring town, agricultural journals, and some magazines of national circulation; a piano stands in the parlor; and perhaps a college pennant or two hang somewhere, for many farm boys and girls go to college.   In spite of the short terms of the public schools, many manage to get some sort of preparation for college, and in the South more college students come from farm homes than from town or city.  This encouraging picture is true, no less than the other, and the number of such progressive farm homes is fortunately growing larger.

A greater range of products is being cultivated

throughout the South, though more cotton and tobacco are being produced than ever before. The output of corn, wheat, hay, and pork has increased in recent years, though the section is not yet self-sufficient. The growing of early vegetables and fruits for Northern markets is a flourishing industry in some sections where land supposedly almost worthless has been found to be admirably adapted for this purpose. An increasing acreage in various legumes not only furnishes forage but enriches the soil. Silos are to be seen here and there, and there are some excellent herds of dairy cattle, though the scarcity of reliable labor makes this form of farming hazardous. The cattle tick is being conquered, and more beef is being produced. Thoroughbred hogs and poultry are common.

With the great rise in the price of the farmer's products since 1910, the man who farms with knowledge and method is growing prosperous. Farmers are taking advantage of the Federal Farm Loan Act and are paying off many mortgages. The necessity of asking for credit is diminishing, and men have contracted to buy land and have paid for it from the first crop. While the things the farmer must buy have risen in price, his products have risen even higher in value; and in those sections of the South suited to mixed farming there need be comparatively little outgo.

One is tempted to hope that the lane has turned for the Southern farmer. Partly owing to his ignorance and inertia, partly to circumstances difficult to overcome, his lot after 1870 was not easy, and from 1870 to 1910 is a full generation. An individual who grew to manhood on a Southern farm during that period may be excused for a gloomy outlook upon the world. He finds it difficult to believe that prosperity has arrived, or that it will last. The number who have been convinced of the brighter outlook, however, is increasing.

# CHAPTER V

## INDUSTRIAL DEVELOPMENT

THOUGH the Old South was in the main agricultural, it was not entirely destitute of industrial skill. The recent industrial development is really a revival, not a revolution, in some parts of the South. In 1810, according to Tench Coxe's semi-official *Statement of Arts and Manufactures*, the value of the textile products of North Carolina was greater than that of Massachusetts. Every farmhouse had spinning-wheels and one loom or several on which the women of the family spun yarn and wove cloth for the family wardrobe. On the large plantations negro women produced much of the cloth for both slaves and family. Except on special occasions, a very large proportion of the clothing worn by the average Southern community was of household or local manufacture. Hats were made of fur, wool, or plaited straw. Hides were tanned on the plantations or more commonly at a local tannery and were made into shoes by local cobblers, white or black.

Local cabinet-makers made furniture, all of it strong, and some of it good in line and finish. Many of the pieces sold by dealers in antiques in the great cities as coming from Europe by way of the South were made by cabinet-makers in Southern villages in the first half of the nineteenth century. Farm wagons as well as carriages with some pretensions to elegance were made in local shops. In fact, up to 1810 or 1820 it seemed that the logical development of one or two of the South Atlantic States would be into frugal manufacturing commonwealths. Few of the thousands of small shops developed into real manufacturing establishments, however, though many continued to exist. The belief in the profits apparently to be made from the cultivation of cotton and tobacco changed the ideals of the people. To own a plantation on which he might lead a patriarchal existence became the ambition of the successful man. Even the lawyer, the doctor, or the merchant was likely to own a plantation to which he expected to retire, if indeed he did not already live on it while he engaged in his other occupation. As the century went on, the section began to depend more and more upon other parts of the country or upon Europe to supply its wants, and general interest in Southern industries began to wane.

Textile establishments had appeared early in the century. The first cotton mill in North Carolina was built in 1810 and one in Georgia about the same time. Much of the machinery for the former was built by local workmen. Other mills were built in the succeeding years until in 1860 there were about 160 in the Southern States, with 300,000 spindles, and a yearly product worth more than $8,000,000. The establishments were small, less than one-third the average size of the mills in New England, and few attempted to supply more than the local demand for coarse yarn which the country women knit into socks or wove into cloth. The surplus was peddled from wagons in adjoining counties or even in a neighboring State. Little attempt was made to seek a wider outlet, and many of these mills could supply the small local demand by running only a few months in the year.

During the Civil War, however, these mills were worked to their full capacity. At the cessation of hostilities many mills were literally worn out; others were destroyed by the invading armies; and fewer were in operation in 1870 than before the War. During the next decade, hope of industrial success began to return to the South.  The mills in operation were making some money; the high price of cotton had brought money into the section; and a few men had saved enough to revive the industry. Old mills were enlarged, and new mills were built. The number in operation in 1880 was about the same as in 1860, but the number of spindles was nearly twice as great.

The Cotton Exposition at Atlanta in 1881 and the New Orleans Exposition in 1884 gave an impetus to the construction of mills.  There were prophecies of future success in the industry, though some self-appointed guardians of the South proved, to their own satisfaction at least, that neither the section nor the people were adapted to the manufacture of cotton and that all their efforts should be devoted to the production of raw material for the mills of New England.  Difficulties were magnified and advantages were minimized by those whose interests were opposed to Southern industrial development, but the movement had now gained momentum and was not to be stopped.  Timidly and hesitantly, capital for building mills was scraped together in dozens of Southern communities, and the number of spindles was doubled between 1880 and 1885 and continued to increase.

In developing this Southern industry there were many difficulties to be overcome, and mistakes were sometimes made. Seduced by apparent cheapness, many of the new mills bought machinery which the New England mills had discarded for better patterns, or because of a change of product. Operatives had to be drawn from the farms and needed to be trained not only to work in the mills but also to habits of regularity and punctuality. The New England overseers who were imported for this purpose sometimes failed in dealing with these new recruits to industrialism because of inability to make due allowance for their limitations. Accustomed to the truck system in agriculture, the managers often paid wages in scrip always good for supplies at the company store but redeemable in cash only at infrequent intervals. The operatives therefore sometimes found that they had exchanged one sort of economic dependence for another. Another difficulty was that a place for Southern yarn and Southern cloth had to be gained in the market, and this was difficult of accomplishment for the product was often not up to the Northern standard.

Managing ability, however, was found not to be

so rare in the South as had been supposed. Some of the managers, drawn perhaps from the village store, the small town bank, or the farm, succeeded so well in the broader field that others were encouraged to seek similar industrial success. As the construction of new mills went on, the temper of the South Atlantic States began to change. The people began to believe in Southern industrial development and to be eager to invest their savings in something other than a land mortgage. An instalment plan by which the savings of the people, small individually but large in the aggregate, were united, furnished capital for mills in scores of towns and villages. In 1890 there were nearly a million and three-quarters spindles in the South compared with less than six hundred thousand ten years before.

It seemed as though nearly every mill was profitable, and the occasional failures did not seriously check the movement, which developed about 1900 almost into a craze in some parts of the South. In these sections every town talked of building one mill or more. The machine shops of the North, which had been cold or at least indifferent to Southern development, woke up, as Southern mills began to double or triple their equipment out of their profits. Agents were sent to the South to encourage the building of new mills, and to give advice and aid in planning them. The new mill-owners were good customers. They had learned wisdom by the mistakes of the pioneers, and they demanded the best machinery with all the latest devices. Long credit was now freely offered by Northern manufacturers of machinery, and some of them even subscribed for stock — to be paid, of course, in machinery.

The Northern textile manufacturers also woke up. They found that in coarse yarns the Southern mills were successfully competing with their products. Some pessimistic representatives of the industry in the North prophesied that the Southern mills would soon control the market. Some New England mills built branch mills in the South; some turned to the finer yarns; and some sought to throw obstacles in the way of their competitors. It has been freely charged by many Southerners that New England manufacturers bore the expense of labor organizers in an unsuccessful attempt to unionize the Southern mill operatives. It has also been charged that the propaganda for legislation restricting the hours of labor and the age of operatives in Southern mills was financed to some extent by New

England manufacturers, and that the writers of the many lurid accounts purporting to describe conditions in Southern mills received pay from the same source.

The system of paying for stock on the instalment plan permitted the construction of many mills for which capital could not have been raised otherwise and had also certain distinct social consequences. According to this plan, the subscriptions to the stock were made payable in weekly instalments of 50 cents or $1.00 a share, thus requiring approximately two or four years to complete payment. Those having money in hand might pay in full, less six per cent discount for the average time. Since almost or quite a year was usually necessary to build the mill and the necessary tenements for the hands, the instalments more than paid this item of expense. The weekly receipts and the payments in full were kept in a local bank, which also expected future business and was therefore likely to be liberal when credit was demanded. Often the officers and directors of the bank were also personally interested in the new enterprise. The machinery manufacturers gave long credit and often took stock in the mill. Commission houses which sold yarns and cloth also took stock with the expectation of controlling the marketing of the product.

Many mills built on this plan were so profitable that they were able to pay for a considerable part of the machinery from the profits long before the last instalment was paid, and some even paid a dividend or two in addition. Such mills started operations with many things in their favor. The ownership was widely distributed, since it was not at all uncommon for a hundred thousand dollar mill to have a hundred or more stockholders, some of whom held only one or two shares. Further, since the amount of money paid in the immediate neighborhood for wages, fuel, and raw material was large, every one was disposed to aid the enterprise in every way possible. Town limits were often changed almost by common consent in order to throw a mill outside so that it would not be subject to town taxes. Where the state constitutions permitted, taxes on the mill were even remitted for a term of years. Where this could not be done, assessors were lenient and usually assessed mill property at much less than its real value.

Not only did some Northern corporations build branch mills in the South, but a considerable amount of Northern capital was invested in mills

Bravura Anderson-Lamb Co N.Y.

under the management of Southern men. It is of course impossible to discover the residence of every stockholder, but enough is known to support the assertion that the proportion of Northern capital is comparatively small. The greater part of the investment in Southern mills has come from the savings of Southern people or has been earned by the mills themselves. Lately several successful mills have been bought by large department stores and mail-order houses, in order to supply them with goods either for the counter directly or else for the manufacture of sheets, pillowcases, underwear, and the like. Marshall Field and Company of Chicago, for example, own several mills in North Carolina.

The mills of the South have continued to increase until they are now much more numerous than in the North. They are smaller in size, however, for in 1915 the number of spindles in the cotton-growing States was 12,711,000 compared with 19,396,-000 in all other States. The consumption of cotton was nevertheless much greater in the South and amounted to 3,414,000 bales, compared with 2,770,-000 bales in the other States. This difference is explained by the fact that Southern mills generally spin coarser yarn and may therefore easily consume twice or even three times as much cotton as mills of the same number of spindles engaged in spinning finer yarn. Some Southern mills, however, spin very fine yarn from either Egyptian or sea-island cotton, but time is required to educate a considerable body of operatives competent to do the more delicate tasks, while less skillful workers are able to produce the coarser numbers.

Southern mills have paid high dividends in the past and have also greatly enlarged their plants from their earnings. They had, years ago, several advantages, some of which persist to the present day. The cost of the raw material was less where a local supply of cotton could be obtained, since freight charges were saved by purchase in the neighborhood; land and buildings for plant and tenements cost less than in the North; fuel was cheaper; water power was often utilized, though sometimes this saving was offset by the cost of transportation; taxes were lower; the rate of wages was lower; there was little or no restriction of the conditions of employment; and there were comparatively few labor troubles.

With the great growth of the industry, however, some of these early advantages have disappeared. Many mills can no longer depend upon the local supply of cotton, and the freight charge from the Lower South is as high as the rate by water to New England or even higher; the transportation of the finished product to Northern markets is an additional expense; wages have risen with the growth of the industry and are approaching closely, if they have not reached, the rate per unit of product paid in other sections. The cost of fuel has increased, although in some localities the development of hydro-electric power has reduced this item. All the States have imposed restrictions upon the employment of women and children in the mills, particularly at night. On the other hand, taxes remain lower, the cost of building is less, and strikes and other forms of industrial friction are still uncommon. When well managed, the Southern mills are still extremely profitable, but margin for error in management has become less.

The Southern mills are chiefly to be found in four States, North Carolina, South Carolina, Georgia, and Alabama, and in the hill country of these States, though a few large mills are situated in the lowlands. North Carolina, with over three hundred mills, has more than any other State, North or South, and consumes more cotton than any other Southern State — over a million bales.

7

South Carolina, however, has more spindles, the average size of its mills is larger, and it spins more fine yarn. North Carolina is second only to Massachusetts in the value of its cotton products, South Carolina comes third, Georgia fourth, and Alabama eighth. Virginia and Tennessee are lower on the list. In quantity of cotton consumed, the cotton growing States passed all others in 1905; and in 1916 the consumption was twenty-five per cent greater, in spite of the fact that New England had been increasing her spindles. Some Southern mills are built in cities, but usually they are in the smaller towns and in little villages which have grown up around the mills and owe their existence to them. There is some localization of industry: a very large number of mills, for instance, may be found in a radius of one hundred miles from Charlotte, North Carolina, and one North Carolina county has more than fifty mills, though the total number of spindles in that county is not much greater than in some single New England establishment.

In the allied knitting industry the production of the South is increasing in importance. North Carolina led the South in 1914, with Tennessee, Georgia, Virginia, following in the order named. Though most of the establishments are small, some are important and are establishing a wide reputation for their product. Generally they are situated in the towns where cotton mills have already been located.

The textile industry, though it is the most important, is not the only great industrial enterprise in the New South. Two others, both in a way the by-products of cotton, deserve attention. Only a few years ago cotton seed was considered a nuisance. A small quantity was fed to stock; a somewhat larger quantity was composted with stable manure and used for fertilizer; but the greater part was left to rot or was even dumped into the streams which ran the gins. Since the discovery of the value of cottonseed products, the industry has grown rapidly. The oil is now used in cooking, is mixed with olive oil, is sold pure for salad oil, and is an important constituent of oleomargarine, lard substitutes, and soap, to name only a few of the uses to which it is put. The cake, or meal from which the oil has been pressed, is rich in nitrogen and is therefore valuable as fertilizer; it is also a standard food for cattle, and tentative experiments with it have even been made as a food for human beings. The hulls have also considerable value as cattle food, and from them are obtained annually nearly a million bales of "linters," that is, short fibers of cotton which escaped the gin. Since the seed is bulky and the cost of transportation is correspondingly high, there are many small cotton-seed oil mills rather than a few large ones. Texas is the leader in this industry, with Georgia next, though oil mills are to be found in all the cotton States, and the value of the seed adds considerably to the income of every cotton grower. In 1914 the value of cottonseed products was $212,000,000.

The industry of making fertilizer depends largely upon cottonseed meal. More than a hundred oil mills have fertilizer departments. The phosphate deposits of the South Atlantic States are also important, and the fertilizer industry is showing more and more a tendency to become sectional. Georgia easily leads, Maryland is second, and no Northern State ranks higher than seventh.

From the standpoint of values lumbering is a more important industry than the manufacture of fertilizers. In this respect Louisiana is the second State in value of products, and the industry is important in Arkansas, Mississippi, and North Carolina. The South furnishes nearly half of the lumber produced in the United States. This industry is, of course, only one step from the raw material.

The manufacture of wood into finished articles is, however, increasing in some of the Southern States. The vehicle industry is considerable, and the same may be said of agricultural machinery, railway and street cars, and coffins. North Carolina especially is taking rank in the manufacture of furniture, most of it cheap but some of it of high grade. So far, ambition has in few cases gone beyond utilization of the native woods, some of which are surprisingly beautiful. Many small establishments in different States make such special products as spokes, shuttle blocks, pails, broom handles, containers for fruits and vegetables, and the like, but the total value of these products is small compared with the value of the crude lumber which is sent out of the South.

The iron industry is important chiefly in Alabama, of the purely Southern States. This State is fourth in the product of its blast furnaces but supplied in 1914 only a little more than six per cent of the total for the United States. Virginia, Tennessee, and West Virginia produce appreciable quantities of pig iron; no Southern State plays a really important part in the steel industry, though Maryland, Alabama, and West Virginia are all represented. Birmingham, Alabama, is the center of steel manufacture and has been called the Pittsburgh of the South, but though the industry has grown rapidly in Birmingham, it has also grown in Pittsburgh, and the Southern city is gaining very slowly. There are great beds of bituminous coal in the South, but only in West Virginia and Alabama is the production really important, though Kentucky, Tennessee, and Virginia produce appreciable quantities.

In the total value of the products of mines of all sorts, West Virginia and Oklahoma are among the leaders, owing to their iron, coal, and petroleum output. Other Southern States follow in the rear. Alabama, Kentucky, Tennessee, Texas, Virginia, Florida, and Louisiana all have a mineral output which is large in the aggregate but a small part of the total. The sulphur mines of Louisiana are growing increasingly important. North Carolina produces a little of almost everything, but its mineral production, except of mica, is not important. In this State large aluminum works have been constructed and the quantity of precious and semiprecious stones found there is a large part of the production for the United States.

The tobacco industry is growing rapidly in the South. There have always been small establishments for the manufacture of tobacco, and many of these during the last three decades have grown to large proportions. New establishments have been opened, some of which are among the largest in the world. The development of the American Tobacco Company and its affiliated and subsidiary organizations has greatly reduced the number of separate establishments. Many were bought by the combination; their brands were transferred to another factory; and the original establishments were closed as uneconomical. Many other small factories, feeling or fearing the competition, closed voluntarily. But the total production of tobacco has steadily increased. Plug and smoking tobacco are largely confined to the Upper South. North Carolina easily leads, while Virginia, Kentucky, and Missouri (if it be classed as a Southern State) also have factories which are known all over the world. Richmond, St. Louis, Louisville, and New Orleans, and Winston-Salem and Durham in North Carolina are the cities which lead in this industry. Winston-Salem probably now makes more plug, and Durham more smoking tobacco, than any other cities in the United States, and the cigarette production of the former is increasing enormously. Some factories supply export trade almost exclusively. There has been little development of the fine cigar industry except in Louisiana and Florida, though in all cities of the Lower South there are local establishments for the manufacture of cigars from Cuban leaf. Richmond is a center for the manufacture of domestic cigars and cheroots and has one mammoth establishment.

Twenty years or thirty years ago scattered over the South there were thousands of small grist mills which ground the farmer's wheat or corn between stones in the old-fashioned way. These are being superseded by roller mills, some of them quite large, which handle all the local wheat and even import some from the West. However, as the annual production of wheat in the South has decreased rather than increased since 1880, it is obvious that the industry has changed in form rather than increased in importance.

There are other less important manufacturing enterprises in the South. The census shows about two hundred and fifty distinct industries pursued to a greater or less extent. Maryland ranked fourteenth in the total value of manufactured products in 1914. Only seven Southern States were found in the first twenty-five, while Minnesota, which is generally considered an agricultural State, ranked higher in manufactures than any of

the Southern group in 1914.   The next census will
undoubtedly give some Southern States high rank,
though the section as a whole is not yet industrial.
The manufacturing output is increasing with mar-
velous rapidity, but it is increasing in other sections of the country as well.   Although the South
was credited in 1914 with an increase of nearly 72
per cent in the value of its products during the
decade, its proportion of the total value of products
in the United States as a whole increased only
from 12.8 per cent in 1904 to 13.1 per cent in 1914.
The section is still far from equaling or surpassing
other sections except in the manufacture of textiles.

# CHAPTER VI

## LABOR CONDITIONS

THE laborer employed in the manufacturing enterprises of the South, whether white or black, is native born and Southern born. Sporadic efforts to import industrial workers from Europe have not been successful and there has been no considerable influx of workers from other sections of the Union. A few skilled workers have come, but the rank and file in all the factories and shops were born in the State in which they work or in a neighboring State. Speaking broadly, those dealing with complicated machines are white, while those engaged in simpler processes are white or black. We find, therefore, a preponderance of whites in the textile industries and in the shops producing articles from wood and iron, while the blacks are found in the lumber industry, in the tobacco factories, in the mines, and at the blast furnaces. There are some skilled workmen among the negroes, especially in tobacco, but generally they furnish the unskilled labor.

The textile industry employs the greatest number of operatives, or at least concentrates them more.   From the farms or the mountain coves, or only one generation removed from that environment, they have been drawn to the mills by various motives.   The South is still sparsely settled, and the life of the tenant farmer or the small landowner and his family is often lonely.   Until recently, roads were almost universally bad, especially in winter, and a visit to town or even to a neighbor was no small undertaking.   Attendance at the country church, which sometimes has services only once a month, or a trip to the country store on Saturday afternoon with an occasional visit to the county-seat furnish almost the only opportunity for social intercourse.   Work in a cotton mill promised not merely fair wages but what was coveted even more — companionship.

During the period of most rapid growth in the textile industry, agriculture, or at least agriculture as practiced by this class, was unprofitable.   During the decade from 1890 to 1900 the price of all kinds of farm produce was exceedingly low, and the returns in money were very small.   Even though a farmer more farsighted than the average did produce the greater part of his food on the farm, his "money crop" — cotton or tobacco — hardly brought the cost of production. The late D. A. Tompkins, of Charlotte, North Carolina, a close student of cotton, came to the conclusion, about 1910, that cotton had been produced at a loss in the South considered as a whole, at least since the Civil War. Many farmers, however, were in a vicious economic circle and could not escape. If they had bought supplies at the country store at inflated prices, the crops sometimes were insufficient to pay the store accounts, and the balance was charged against the next year's crop. Men who did not go heavily into debt often handled less than $200 in cash in a year, and others found difficulty in obtaining money even for their small taxes. To such men the stories of $15 to $25 earned at a mill by a single family in a week seemed almost fabulous. The whole family worked on the farm, as farmers' families have always done, and it seemed the natural thing that, in making a change, all should work in the mill.

To those families moved by loneliness and those other families driven by an honest ambition to better their economic condition were added the families of the incapable, the shiftless, the disabled, and the widowed. In a few cases men came to the mills deliberately intending to exploit their children, to live a life of ease upon their earnings. There were places for the younger members of all these families, but a man with hands calloused and muscles stiffened by the usual round of farm work could seldom learn a new trade after the age of forty, no matter how willing. Often a cotton mill is the only industrial enterprise in the village, and the number of common laborers needed is limited. Too many of the fathers who had come to the village intending themselves to work gradually sank into the parasite class and sat around the village store while their children worked.

During the early expansion of the industry, the wages paid were low compared with New England standards, but they were sufficient to draw the people from the farms and to hold them at the mills. In considering the wages paid in Southern mills, this fact must never be forgotten. There was always an abundance of land to which the mill people could return at will and wrest some sort of living from the soil. For them to go back to the land was not a venture full of unknown hazards. They had been born on the land and even yet are usually only one generation removed, and the land cries out for tenants and laborers. It must also be remembered that though the wages measured in money were low, the cost of living was likewise low. Rents were trifling, if indeed the tenements were not occupied free; the cost of fuel and food was low; and many expenses necessary in New England were superfluous in the South.

With the increasing number of mills and the rising price of agricultural products, the supply of industrial laborers became less abundant, and higher wages have been necessary to draw recruits from the farms until at present the rate of wages approaches that of New England. The purchasing power is probably greater for, while the cost of living has greatly increased in the South, it is still lower than in other parts of the country. This does not mean that the average Southern wage is equal to the New England average. While there is a growing body of highly skilled operatives in the South, the rapid growth of the industry has made necessary the employment of an overwhelmingly large number of untrained or partially trained operatives, who cannot tend so many spindles or looms as the New England operatives. Again, much yarn in the North is spun upon mules, while in the South these machines are uncommon. For certain purposes, this soft but fine and even yarn is indispensable. Only strong, highly skilled operatives, usually men, can tend these machines. The earnings of such specialists cannot fairly be compared with the amounts received by ordinary girl spinners on ring frames. Again the weekly wage of an expert weaver upon fancy cloth cannot justly be compared with that of a Southern operative upon plain goods. Where the work is comparable, however, the rates per unit of product in North and South are not far apart.

From the standpoint of the employer it may be possible that the wages per unit of product are higher in some Southern mills than in some New England establishments. In the case of an expensive machine, an operative who gets from it only sixty to seventy-five per cent of its possible production may receive higher wages, or what amounts to the same thing, may produce at a higher cost per unit than a more highly paid individual who more nearly approaches the theoretical maximum production of the machine. There is much expensive machinery in the Southern mills. In fact, on the whole, the machinery for the work in hand is better than in New England, because it is newer. The

recently built Southern mills have been equipped
with all the latest machinery, while many of the
older Northern mills have not felt able to scrap
machines which, though antiquated, were still running well.  However, the advantage in having a
better machine is not fully realized if it is not run
to its full capacity.  Both spinning frames and
looms have generally been run at a somewhat
slower speed in the South than in the North.  This
fact was noted by that careful English observer,
T. M. Young: "Whether the cost per unit of efficiency is greater in the South than in the North
is hard to say.  But for the automatic loom, the
North would, I think, have the advantage.  Perhaps the truth is that in some parts of the South
where the industry has been longest established
and a generation has been trained to the work,
Southern labor is actually as well as nominally
cheaper than Northern; whilst in other districts,
where many mills have sprung up all at once
amongst a sparse rural population, wholly untrained, the Southern labor at present procur-
able is really dearer than the Northern."[1]  This
does not mean that Southern labor is permanently inferior; but a highly skilled body of

[1] T. M. Young, *The American Cotton Industry*, p. 113.

operatives requires years for its development.
In the beginning there were no restrictions upon
hours of work, age, or sex of operatives, or conditions of employment. Every mill was a law unto
itself. Hours were long, often seventy-two and in
a few cases seventy-five a week. Wages were often
paid in scrip good at the company store but redeemable in cash only at infrequent intervals, if
indeed any were then presented. Yet, if the prices
at the store were sometimes exorbitant, they were
likely to be less than the operatives had been accustomed to pay when buying on credit while living on the farms. The moral conditions at some of
these mills were also bad, since the least desirable element of the rural population was the first to go to
the mills. Such conditions, however, were not universal. Some of the industrial communities were
clean and self-respecting, but conditions depended
largely upon the individual in charge of the mill.

As the years went on and more and more mills
were built, the demand for operatives increased.
To draw them from the farms, it was necessary to
improve living conditions in the mill villages and
to increase wages. Today the mill communities
are generally clean, and care is taken to exclude
immoral individuals. Payment of wages in cash

8

became the rule. The company store persisted, but chiefly as a matter of convenience to the operatives; and in prices it met and often cut below those charged in other stores in the vicinity. The hours of labor were reduced gradually. Seventy-two became the maximum, but most mills voluntarily ran sixty-nine or even sixty-six. The employment of children continued, though some individual employers reduced it as much as possible without seriously crippling their forces. This was a real danger so long as there were no legal restrictions on child labor. Children worked upon the farm as children have done since farming began, and the average farmer who moved to the mill was unable to see the difference between working on the farm and working in the mill. In fact, to his mind, work in the mill seemed easier than exposure on the farm to the summer sun and the winter cold.

Men who were not conscious of deliberately exploiting their children urged the manager of the mill to employ a child of twelve or even ten. If the manager refused, he was threatened with the loss of the whole family. A family containing good operatives could always find employment elsewhere, and perhaps the manager of another mill would not be so scrupulous. So the children went into the mill and often stayed there. If illiterate when they entered, they remained illiterate. The number of young children, however, was always exaggerated by the muckrakers, though unquestionably several hundred children ten to twelve years old, and possibly a few younger, were employed years ago. The nature of the work permits the employment of operatives under sixteen only in the spinning room; the girls, many of them older than sixteen, mend the broken ends of the yarn at the spinning frames, and the boys remove the full bobbins and fix empty ones in their stead. The possible percentage of workers under sixteen in a spinning mill varies from thirty-five to forty-five. In a mill which weaves the yarn into cloth, the percentage is greatly reduced, as practically no one under sixteen can be profitably employed in a weaving room.

Public sentiment against the employment of children became aroused only slowly. Crusades against such industrial customs are usually led by organized labor, by professional philanthropists, by sentimentalists, and by socialistic agitators. The mill operatives of the South have shown little disposition to organize themselves and, in fact, have protested against interference with their right of contract. The South is only just becoming rich enough to support professional philanthropists, and an outlet for sentimentality has been found in other directions. There has been as yet too little disproportion of wealth among the Southern whites to excite acute jealousy on this ground alone, and the operatives have earned much more money in the mills than was possible on the farms. In comparatively few cases does one man, or one family, own a controlling interest in a mill. The ownership is usually scattered in small holdings, and there is seldom a Crœsus to excite envy. This wide ownership has had its effect upon the general attitude of the more influential citizens and hindered the development of active disapproval.

The chief reason for the inertia in labor matters, however, has been the fact that the South has thought, and to a large extent still thinks, in terms of agriculture. It has not yet developed an industrial philosophy. Agriculture is individualistic, and Thomas Jefferson's ideas upon the functions and limitations of government still have influence. Regulation of agricultural labor would seem absurd, and the difference between a family, with or without hired help, working in comparative freedom on a farm, and scores of individuals working at the same tasks, day after day, under more or less tension was slow to take shape in the popular consciousness. It was obvious that the children were not actually physically abused; almost unanimously they preferred work to school, just as the city boy does today; and the children themselves opposed most strongly any proposed return to the farm. The task of the reformers — for in every State there were earnest men and women who saw the evils of unrestricted child labor — was difficult. It was the same battle which had been fought in England and later in New England, when their textile industries were passing through the same stage of development. Every student of industrial history realizes that conditions in the South were neither so hard nor were the hours so long as they had been in England and New England.

The attempt to apply pressure from without had little influence. Indeed it is possible that the resentment occasioned by the exaggerated stories of conditions really hindered the progress of restrictive legislation, just as the bitter denunciation of the Southern attitude toward the negro has increased conservatism. Every one knew that the pitiful stories of abuse or oppression were untrue. No class of laborers anywhere is more independent than Southern mill operatives. It has been a long while since a family of even semi-efficient operatives has been compelled to ask for employment. Runners for other mills, upon the slightest hint of disaffection, are quick to seek them out and even to advance the expense of moving and money to pay any debts. It is well known that families move for the slightest reason or for no reason at all except a vague unrest. Self-interest, if nothing else, would restrain an overseer from an act which might send a whole family or perhaps half a dozen families from his mill.

Gradually the States imposed limitations upon age of employment, hours of labor, and night work for women and children, which practically meant limiting or abolishing night work altogether. These restrictions were slight at first, and the provisions for their enforcement were inadequate, but succeeding legislatures increased them. Mild compulsory attendance laws kept some of the children in school and out of the mill. A more or less substantial body of labor legislation was gradually growing up, when state regulation was stopped by the action of the Federal Government. Since the first Federal Child Labor Act was declared unconstitutional, several States have strengthened laws

previously existing, and have further reduced the hours of labor.

Until comparatively recently whatever provision was made for the social betterment of the operatives depended upon the active manager of the particular mill. Some assumed a patriarchal attitude and attempted to provide those things which they thought the operatives should have. Others took little or no responsibility, except perhaps to make a contribution to all the churches represented in the community. This practice is almost universal, and if the term of the public school is short, it is usually extended by a contribution from the mill treasury. During recent years much more has been done. Partly from an awakening sense of social responsibility and partly from a realization that it is good business to do so, the bigger mills have made large expenditures to improve the condition of their operatives. They have provided reading rooms and libraries, have opened many recreation rooms and playgrounds, and have furnished other facilities for entertainment. Some of the mills have athletic fields, and a few support semi-professional baseball teams. At some mills community buildings have been erected, which sometimes contain, in addition to public rooms, baths, and a swimming pool, an office for a visiting nurse and rooms which an adviser in domestic science may use for demonstration. The older women are hard to teach, but not a few of the girls take an interest in the work. Nothing is more needed than instruction in domestic science. The operatives spend a large proportion of their income upon food — for the rent they pay is trifling — but the items are not always well chosen, and the cooking is often bad. To the monotonous dietary to which they were accustomed on the farms they add many luxuries to be had in the mill town, but these are often ruined by improper preparation. Owing to this lack of domestic skill many operatives apparently suffer from malnutrition, though they spend more than enough money to supply an abundance of nourishing food.

Not many years ago the improvidence of the mill operatives was proverbial. Wages were generally spent as fast as they were earned, and often extravagantly. Little attempt was made to cultivate gardens or to make yards attractive, with the result that a factory village with its monotonous rows of unkempt houses was a depressing sight. The "factory people," many of whom had been nomad tenant farmers seldom living long in the same place, had never thought of attempting to beautify their surroundings, and the immediate neighborhood of the mill to which they moved was often bare and unlovely and afforded little encouragement to beauty.

The improvident family is still common, and many ugly mill villages yet exist, but one who has watched the development of the cotton industry in the South for twenty-five years has seen great changes in these respects. Thousands of families are saving money today. Some buy homes; others set up one member of the family in a small business; and a few buy farms. More than seventy-five families have left one mill village during the last ten years to buy farms with their savings, but this instance is rather unusual; comparatively few families return to the land. Efforts have been made to develop a community spirit, and the results are perceptible. Many mill villages are now really attractive. Scores of mills have had their grounds laid out by a landscape architect, and a mill covered with ivy and surrounded by well-kept lawns and flower beds is no longer exceptional. In scores of mill communities annual prizes are offered for the best vegetable garden, the most attractive premises, and the best kept premises from a sanitary standpoint.

The Southern operative is too close to the soil to be either socialistic in his views or collectivistic in his attitude. The labor agitator has found sterile soil for his propaganda. Yet signs of a dawning class consciousness are appearing. As always, the first manifestation is opposition to the dominant political party or faction. This has not yet, however, been translated into any considerable number of Republican votes, except in North Carolina. In the other States, the votes of the factory operatives seem to be cast in something of a block, in the primary elections. The demagogic Blease is said to have found much of his support in South Carolina in the factory villages.

Employees in other industries show so much diversity that few general statements can be made concerning them. The workers in the furniture factories — who are chiefly men, as few women or children can be employed in this industry — are few in number compared with the male employees in the cotton mills and, except in the case of a few towns, can hardly be discussed as a group at all. Both whites and negroes are employed, but the white man is usually in the responsible post, though a few negroes tend important machines. The general average of education and intelligence among the whites is higher here than in the cotton mills, and wages are likewise higher. Conditions in other establishments making articles of wood are practically the same.

Lumber mills range from a small neighborhood sawmill with a handful of employees to the great organizations which push railroads into the deep woods and strip a mountain side or devastate the lowlands. Such organizations require a great number of laborers, whom they usually feed and to whom they issue from a "commissary" various necessary articles which are charged against the men's wages. As the work is hard, it has not been at all uncommon for employees who had received large advances to decamp. The companies, however, took advantage of various laws similar to those mentioned in the chapter on agriculture to have these deserters arrested and to have them, when convicted, "hired out" to the very company or employer from whom they had fled. Conditions resulting from this practice in some of the States of the Lower South became so scandalous about 1905 that numerous individuals were tried in the courts and were convicted of holding employees in a state of peonage. In 1911 the Supreme Court of the United States declared unconstitutional the

law of Alabama regarding contract of service.[1]
This law regarded the nonfulfillment of a contract
on which an advance had been made as *prima facie*
evidence of intent to defraud and thus gave employers immense power over their employees. Conditions have therefore undoubtedly improved since
the peonage trials, but the lumber industry is one
in which the labor has apparently everywhere been
casual, migratory, and lawless.

The manufacture of tobacco shows as much diversity of labor conditions as the lumber industry.
There are small establishments with little machinery which manufacture plug and smoking tobacco
and are open only a few months in the year, as well
as those which cover half a dozen city blocks. In
the smaller factories the majority of the laborers
are black, but in the larger establishments both negroes and whites are employed. Sometimes they
do the same sort of work on opposite sides of the
same room. In some departments negro and white
men work side by side, while in others only whites
or only negroes are found. The more complicated
machines are usually tended by whites, and the
filling and inspection of containers is ordinarily
done by white girls, who are also found in large

[1] Bailey *vs.* Alabama, 219 U. S., 219.

numbers in the cigarette factories. Not many
years ago the tobacco industry was supposed to
belong to the negro, but with the introduction
of machinery he has lost his monopoly, though
on account of the expansion of the industry the
total number of negroes employed is greater than
ever before.

In the smaller factories labor is usually paid by
the day, but in the larger establishments every
operation possible is on a piecework basis. These
operations are so related in a series that a slacker
feels the displeasure of those who follow him and
depend upon him for a supply of material. In the
smaller factories the work is regarded somewhat in
the light of a summer holiday, as the tasks are
simple and the operatives talk and sing at their
work. This social element largely disappears, however, with the introduction of machinery. As
might be expected in a labor force composed of
men, women, and children, both white and black,
with some engaged in manual labor and others tend-
ing complicated machines, there is little solidarity.
An organized strike including any large percentage
of the force in a tobacco factory is a practical im-
possibility. Those engaged in a particular process
may strike and in consequence tie up the processes

depending upon them, but any sort of industrial friction is uncommon. The general level of wages has been steadily rising, and among the negroes the tobacco workers are the aristocrats of the wage earners and are content with their situation. Since the larger factories are almost invariably in the cities, the homes of the workers are scattered and not collected in communities as around the cotton mills.

Experiments have been made in employing negro operatives in the textile industry, so far with little success, though the capacity of the negro for such employment has not yet been disproved. Though several cotton mills which made the experiment failed, in every case there were difficulties which might have caused a similar failure even with white operatives. Negroes have been employed successfully in some hosiery mills and in a few small silk mills. The increasing scarcity of labor, especially during the Great War, has led to the substitution of negroes for whites in a number of knitting mills. Some successful establishments are conducted with negro labor but the labor force is either all white or all black except that white overseers are always, or nearly always employed.

An important hindrance in the way of the success

of negroes in these occupations is their characteristic dislike of regularity and punctuality. As the negro has acquired these virtues to some extent at least in the tobacco industry, there seems to be no reason to suppose that in time he may not succeed also in textiles, in which the work is not more difficult than in other tasks of which negroes have proved themselves capable. So far the whites have not resented the occasional introduction of black operatives into the textile industry. If the negroes become firmly established while the demand for operatives continues to be greater than the supply, race friction on this account is unlikely, but if they are introduced in the future as strikebreakers, trouble is sure to arise. In the mines, blast furnaces, oil mills, and fertilizer factories the negroes do the hardest and most unpleasant tasks, work which in the North is done by recent immigrants.

The negroes are almost entirely unorganized and are likely to remain so for a long time. Few negroes accumulate funds enough to indulge in the luxury of a strike, and they have shown little tendency to organize or support unions. However, their devotion to their lodges shows the loyalty of which they are capable, and their future organization is not beyond the range of possibility. Generally the South has afforded little encouragement to organized labor. Even the white workers, except in the cities and in a few skilled trades, have shown until recently little tendency to organize. In the towns and villages they are not sharply differentiated from the other elements of the population. They look upon themselves as citizens rather than as members of the laboring class. Except in a few of the larger towns one does not hear of "class conflict"; and the "labor vote," when by any chance a Socialist or a labor candidate is nominated, is not large enough to be a factor in the result.

During 1918 and 1919, however, renewed efforts to organize Southern labor met with some success particularly in textile and woodworking establishments, though the tobacco industry and public utilities were likewise affected. The efforts of employers to prevent the formation of unions led to lockouts and strikes during which there was considerable disorder and some bloodshed. Communities which had known of such disputes only from hearsay stood amazed. The workers generally gained recognition of their right to organize, and their success may mean greater industrial friction in the future.

# CHAPTER VII

## THE PROBLEM OF BLACK AND WHITE

FOR a century, the presence of the negro in the
United States has divided the nation. Though the
Civil War finally decided some questions about his
status, others affecting his place in the social order
remained unsettled; new controversies have arisen;
and no immediate agreement is in sight. Interest
in the later phases of the race question has found
expression in scores of books, hundreds of articles,
thousands of orations and addresses, and unlimited private discussions which have generally
produced more heat than light. The question has
kept different sections of the country apart and has
created bitterness which will long endure. Moreover, this discussion about ten million people has
produced an effect upon them, and the negroes are
beginning to feel that they constitute a problem.

Differing attitudes toward the negro generally arise from fundamentally different postulates.

9 129

Many Northerners start with the assumption that the negro is a black Saxon and argue that his faults and deficiencies arise from the oppression he has endured. At the other extreme are those who hold that the negro is fundamentally different from the white man and inferior to him: and some go so far as to say that he is incapable of development. Fifty years ago General John Pope predicted, with a saving reservation, that the negroes of Georgia would soon surpass the whites in education, culture, and wealth. Other predictions, similar in tone, were common in the reports of various philanthropic associations. Obviously these prophecies have not been fulfilled; but it is just as evident that the predictions that the former slaves would relapse into barbarism and starve have also not been realized. Practically every prophecy or generalization made before 1890 with regard to the future of the negro has been discredited by the events of the passing years.

It is perhaps worth while to take stock of what this race has accomplished in America during something more than fifty years of freedom. The negro has lived beside the white man and has increased in numbers, though at a somewhat slower rate than the white. The census of 1870 was inaccurate and incomplete in the South, and in consequence the census of 1880 seemed to show a phenomenal increase in the negro population. Upon this supposed increase was based the theory that the South would soon be overwhelmingly black. From the historical standpoint, Albion W. Tourgée's *Appeal to Caesar* is interesting as a perfect example of this type of deduction, for he could see only a black South. The three censuses taken since 1880 definitely establish the fact that the net increase of negro population is smaller than that of the white. This seems to have been true at every census since 1810, and the proportion of negroes to the total population of the nation grows steadily, though slowly, smaller. [1]

[1] Though the negro increase is smaller than the white, nevertheless the 4,441,930 negroes in 1860 had increased to 9,827,763 in 1910. Of this number 8,749,427 lived in the Southern States, and 1,078,336 in the Northern. That is to say, 89 per cent of the negroes lived in the three divisions classed as Southern, 10.5 per cent in the four divisions classed as Northern and 0.5 per cent in the two Western divisions. Since 1790 the center of negro population has been moving toward the Southwest and has now reached northeast Alabama. Migration to the North and West has been considerable since emancipation. In 1910 there were 415,533 negroes born in the South but living in the North, and, owing to this migration, the percentage of increase of negro population outside the South has been larger than the average. Between 1900 and 1910 the increase in the New England States was 12.2 per cent and in the East North Central 16.7 per cent. The mountain divisions show a large percentage of increase, but as there were in both of them together less than 51,000 negroes, comprising less

Between 1900 and 1910, the native white population increased 20.9 per cent while the negro population increased only 11.2 per cent. This smaller increase in the later decade is due partly to negro migration to the cities. It is believed that among the city negroes, particularly in the North, the death rate is higher than the birth rate. The excessive death rate results largely from crowded and unsanitary quarters.

Since 1910, the migration of negroes to the North has been larger than before. The increase was not unusual, however, until the beginning of the Great War. Up to that time the majority had been engaged in domestic and personal service, but with the practical cessation of immigration from Europe, a considerable number of negro laborers moved to the Northern States. Indeed, in some Southern communities the movement almost reached the proportions of an exodus. Until the next census there is no means of estimating with any approach to accuracy the extent of this migration. The truth is probably somewhere in between the published

than 1 per cent of the population, it is evident that the negro is not a serious factor in the West. The negroes form an insignificant component (less than 5 per cent) of the population of any Northern State, though in some Northern cities the number of negroes is considerable. See *Abstract of the Thirteenth Census of the United States*, p. 78.

estimates which range from 300,000 to 1,000,000. The investigations of the United States Department of Labor indicate the smaller number.

The motives for this northward migration are various. The offer of higher wages is the most important. The desire to get for their children greater educational advantages than are offered in the South is also impelling. The belief that race prejudice is less strong in the North is another inducement to leave the South, for "Jim Crow" cars and political disfranchisement have irritated many. Finally the dread of lynch law may be mentioned as a motive for migration, though its actual importance may be doubted. Not all the negroes who have moved to the North have remained there. Many do not allow for the higher cost of food and shelter in their new home, and these demands upon the higher wages leave a smaller margin than was expected. Others find the climate too severe, while still others are unable or unwilling to work regularly at the speed demanded.

The overwhelming mass of the negro population in the South, and therefore in the nation, is still rural, though among them, as among the whites, the drift toward the cities is marked. The chief occupations are agriculture, general jobbing not requiring skilled labor, and domestic service, although there is a scattered representation of negroes in almost every trade, business, and profession. In 1865 the amount of property held by negroes was small. A few free negroes were upon the tax-books, and former masters sometimes made gifts of property to favorites among the liberated slaves, but the whole amount was trifling compared with the total number of negroes. In 1910, in the Southern States, title to 15,691,536 acres of land was held by negroes, and the equity was large. This amount represents an increase of over 2,330,-000 acres since 1900 but is nevertheless only 4.4 per cent of the total farm land in the South. As tenants or managers, negroes cultivated in addition nearly 27,000,000 acres. In other words, 29.8 per cent of the population owned 4.4 per cent of the land and cultivated 12 per cent of it. The total value of the land owned was $273,000,000, an average of $1250 to the farm.[1]

[1] It must be noted, however, that during the decade ending in 1910, the percentage of increase in negro farm owners was 17 as against 12 for the whites, and of increase in the value of their holdings was 156 per cent as against 116 per cent for whites, while the proportion of white tenants increased. The other property of the negro can only be estimated, as most States do not list the races separately. The census for 1910 reports 430,449 homes, rural and urban, owned by negroes, and of these 314,340 were free of encumbrance, compared with a total of

Speaking broadly, the right of the negro to work at any sort of manual or mechanical labor is not questioned in the South. Negroes and whites work together on the farm, and a negro may rent land almost anywhere. In thousands of villages and towns one may see negro plumbers, carpenters, and masons working by the side of white men. A negro shoemaker or blacksmith may get the patronage of whites at his own shop or may share a shop with a white man. White and negro teamsters are employed indiscriminately. Hundreds of negroes serve as firemen or as engineers of stationary steam engines. Thousands work in the tobacco factories. Practically the only distinction made is this: a negro man may work with white men indoors or out, but he may not work indoors by the side of white women except in some subordinate capacity, as porter or waiter. Occasionally he works with white women out of doors. Lack of economic success therefore cannot be charged entirely or even primarily to racial discrimination. Where the negro often fails is in lack of reliability, regularity, and faithfulness. In some occupations

---

327,537 homes in 1900, of which 229,158 were free. Further discussion of the part of the negro in agriculture will be found in another chapter.

he is losing ground. Not many years ago barbers, waiters, and hotel employees in the South usually were negroes, but they have lost their monopoly in all these occupations. White men are taking their place as barbers and white girls now often serve in dining-rooms and on elevators. On the other hand, the number of negro seamstresses seems to be increasing. A generation ago, many locomotive firemen were negroes, but now the proportion is decreasing. There are hundreds, even thousands, of negro draymen who own teams, and some of them have become prosperous.

White patronage of negroes in business depends partly upon custom and partly upon locality. Negroes who keep livery stables and occasionally garages receive white patronage. In nearly every community there is a negro woman who bakes cakes for special occasions. Many negroes act as caterers or keep restaurants, but these must be for whites only or blacks only, but not for both. A negro market gardener suffers no discrimination, and a negro grocer may receive white patronage, though he usually does not attempt to attract white customers. There are a few negro dairymen, and some get the best prices for their products. Where a negro manufactures or sells goods in a larger way, as in brickyards, cement works, lumber yards and the like, race prejudice does not interfere with his trade.

Negro professional men, on the other hand, get little or no white patronage. No negro pastor preaches to a white congregation, and no negro teaches in a school for whites. Negro lawyers, dentists, and doctors are practically never employed by whites. In the past the number engaged in these professions has been negligible, and that any increase in the total of well trained negro professional men will make an immediate change in the attitude of whites is unlikely. The relation of lawyer and client or physician and patient presumes a certain intimacy and subordination to greater wisdom which the white man is not willing to acknowledge where a negro is involved. Negro women, trained or partially trained, are employed as nurses, however, in increasing numbers.

In 1865, the great mass of negroes was wholly illiterate. Some of the free negroes could read and write, and a few had graduated at some Northern college. Though the laws which forbade teaching slaves to read or write were not generally enforced, only favored house servants received instruction. It is certain that the percentage of illiteracy was at least 90, and possibly as high as 95.   This has been progressively reduced until in 1910 the proportion of the illiterate negro population ten years old or over was 30.4 per cent, and the number of college and university graduates was considerable though the proportion was small.    Since the percentage of native white illiteracy in the United States is but 3, the negro is evidently ten times as illiterate as the native white.   This comparison is not fair to the negro, however, for illiteracy in the urban communities in the United States is less than in the rural districts, owing largely to better educational facilities in the cities; and 82.3 per cent of the negro population is rural.[1]

The negroes along with the whites have suffered and still suffer from the inadequate school facilities of the rural South.    The percentage of illiterate negro children between the ages of ten and fourteen

[1] In New England negro illiteracy is 7.1 per cent in the cities and 16.9 per cent in the rural communities.   Then, too, the great masses of negroes live in States which are predominantly rural and in which the percentage of white illiteracy is also high.   The percentage of native white illiteracy in the rural districts of the South Atlantic States is 9.8 and in the East South Central is 11.1 per cent.   Negro illiteracy in the corresponding divisions is 36.1 per cent and 37.8 per cent.   In the urban communities of these divisions, illiteracy on the part of both whites and negroes is less.   Native white illiteracy is 2.2 per cent and 2.4 per cent respectively, while negro illiteracy in the towns was 21.4 and 23.8 per cent respectively.

in the country as a whole was only 18.9 per cent compared with the general average of 30.4 for the negroes as a whole. It is evident, then, that as the negroes now fifty years old and over die off, the illiteracy of the whole mass will continue to drop, for it is in the older group that the percentage of illiterates is highest. It must not be concluded from these figures that negro illiteracy is not a grave problem, nor that negro ability is equal to that of the whites, nor that the negro has taken full advantage of such opportunities as have been open to him. It does appear, however, that the proportion of negro illiteracy is not entirely his fault.

The negro fleeing from discrimination in the South has not always found a fraternal welcome in the North, for the negro mechanic has generally been excluded from white unions and has often been denied the opportunity to work at his trade.[1] He has also found difficulty in obtaining living accommodations and there has been much race friction. It is perhaps a question worth asking whether any considerable number of white men of Northern European stock are without an instinctive dislike of those manifestly unlike themselves.

[1] The American Federation of Labor in 1919 voted to take steps to recognize and admit negro unions.

The history of the contact between such stocks and the colored races shows instance after instance of refusal to recognize the latter as social or political equals. Indian, East Indian, and African have all been subjected to the domination of the whites. There have been many cases of illicit mating, of course, but the white man has steadily refused to legitimize these unions. The South European, on the contrary, has mingled freely with the natives of the countries he has colonized and to some extent has been swallowed up by the darker mass. Mexico, Brazil, Cuba, the Portuguese colonies in different parts of the world, are obvious examples.[1]

In the Southern States the white man has made certain decisions regarding the relation of blacks and whites and is enforcing them without regard to the negro's wishes. The Southerner is convinced that the negro is inferior and acts upon that conviction. There is no suggestion that the laws forbidding intermarriage be repealed, or that separate schools be discontinued. Restaurants and hotels

[1] How much of this difference in attitude is due to lack of pride in race integrity and how much to religion is a question. The Roman Catholic Church, which is dominant in Southern Europe, does not encourage such inter-racial marriages, but, on the other hand, it does not forbid them or pronounce them unlawful. Yet this cannot explain the whole difference. There seems to be another factor.

must cater to one race only. Most of the States require separation of the races in common carriers and even in railway stations. The laws require that "equal accommodations" shall be furnished on railroads, but violations are frequently evident, as the railways often assign old or inferior equipment to the negroes. In street cars one end is often assigned to negroes and the other to whites, and therefore the races alternate in the use of the same seats when the car turns back at the end of the line. The division in a railway station may be nothing more than a bar or a low fence across the room, and one ticket office with different windows may serve both races.

Some of these regulations are defended on the ground that by reducing close contact they lessen the chances of race conflict. That such a result is measurably attained is probable, and the comfort of traveling is increased for the whites at least. William Archer, the English journalist and author, in *Through Afro-America* says, "I hold the system of separate cars a legitimate means of defence against constant discomfort," and most travelers will approve his verdict. The chief reason for such regulations, however, is to assert and emphasize white superiority. Half a dozen black nurses with their charges may sit in the car reserved for whites, because they are obviously dependents engaged in personal service. Without such relationship, however, not one of them would be allowed to remain. It is not so much the presence of the negro to which the whites object but to that presence in other than an inferior capacity. This is the explanation of much of the so-called race prejudice in the South: it is not prejudice against the individual negro but is rather a determination to assert white superiority. So long as the negro is plainly dependent and recognizes that dependency, the question of prejudice does not arise, and there is much kindly intimacy between individuals. The Southern white man or white woman of the better class is likely to protect and help many negroes at considerable cost of time, labor, and money, but the relationship is always that of superior and inferior. If a suggestion of race equality creeps in, antagonism is at once aroused.

It is the fashion to speak of the "old-time negro" and the "new negro." The types are easily recognizable. One is quiet, unobtrusive, more or less industrious. He "knows his place" — which may mean anything from servility to self-respecting acceptance of his lot in life. The other resents more or less openly the discrimination against his race, and this resentment may range from impertinence to sullenness and even to dreams of social equality imposed by force. Some have a smattering of education while others, who have been subjected to little training or discipline, are indolent and shiftless. The thoughtless, however, are likely to include in this classification the industrious, intelligent negro who orders his conduct along the same lines as the white man.

This last type, it is true, is sometimes regarded with suspicion. Many men and women in the South fear the progress of the negro. They do not realize that the South cannot really make satisfactory progress while any great proportion of the population is relatively inefficient. Some fear the negro's demand to be treated as a man. On the other hand, many negroes demand to be treated as men, while ignoring or perhaps not realizing the fact that, to be treated as a man, one must play a man's part. As Booker Washington put the matter, many are more interested in getting recognition than in getting something to recognize. Many are much more interested in their rights than in their duties. To be sure the negro is not alone in this, for the same attitude is to be found in immigrants coming from the socially and politically backward states of Europe. The ordinary negro, however, apparently does not think much of such problems of the future, though no white man is likely to know precisely what he does think. He goes about his business or his pleasure seemingly at peace with the world, though perhaps he sings somewhat less than he once did. He attends his church and the meetings of his lodge or lodges, and works more or less regularly. Probably the great majority of negroes more nearly realize their ambitions than do the whites. They do not aspire to high position, and discrimination does not burn them quite as deeply as the sometimes too sympathetic white man who tries to put himself in their place may think.

There are, however, some individuals to whom the ordinary conditions of any negro's life appear particularly bitter. With mental ability, education, and æsthetic appreciation often comparable to those of the whites, and with more than normal sensitiveness, they find the color line an intolerable insult, since it separates them from what they value most. They rage at the barrier which shuts them out from the society which they feel themselves qualified to enter, and they are always on the alert to discern injuries. These injuries need not be positive, for neglect is quite as strong a grievance.

These individuals all spell negro with a capital and declare that they are proud of their race. They parade its achievements — and these are not small when enumerated all at once — but they avoid intimate association with the great mass of negroes. They are not at all democratic, and in a negro state they would assume the privileges of an aristocracy as a matter of right. It would seem that their demand for full political and social rights for all negroes has for its basis not so much the welfare of the race as a whole, as the possibility of obtaining for themselves special privileges and positions of leadership. They are not satisfied merely with full legal rights. In those States where there is no legal discrimination in public places, their denunciation of social prejudice is bitter. They are not content to take their chances with other groups but sometimes are illogical enough to demand social equality enforced by law, though by this phrase they mean association with the whites merely for themselves; they do not wish other negroes less developed than themselves to associate with them.

In any city where there is any considerable number of this class, there is a section of negro society

10

in which social lines are drawn as strictly as in the most aristocratic white community. To prove that the negroes are not emotional, these aristocrats among them are likely to insist upon rigid formality in their church services and upon meticulous correctness in all the details of social gatherings. Since many of these individuals have a very large admixture of white blood, occasionally one crosses the barrier and "goes white." Removal to a new town or city gives the opportunity to cut loose from all previous associations and to start a new life. The transition is extremely difficult, of course, and requires much care and discretion, but it has been made. The greater part of them nevertheless remain negroes in the eyes of the law, however much they strive to separate themselves in thought and action from the rest of their kind. It is this small class of "intellectuals" who were Booker T. Washington's bitterest enemies. His theory that the negro should first devote himself to obtaining economic independence and should leave the adjustment of social relations to the future was denounced as treason to the race. Washington's opportunism was even more obnoxious to them than is the superior attitude of the whites. They denounced him as a trimmer, a time-server, and a traitor, and on occasion they hissed him from the platform. From their safe refuges in Northern cities, some negro orators and editors have gone so far as to advocate the employment of the knife and the torch to avenge real or fancied wrongs, but these counsels have done little harm for they have not been read by those to whom they were addressed. Perhaps, indeed, they may not have been meant entirely seriously, for the negro, like other emotional peoples, sometimes plays with words without realizing their full import.

On the whole there is surprisingly little friction between the blacks and the whites. One may live a long time in many parts of the South without realizing that the most important problem of the United States lies all about him. Then an explosion comes, and he realizes that much of the South is on the edge of a volcano. For a time the white South attempted to divest itself of responsibility for the negro. He had turned against those who had been his friends and had followed after strange gods; therefore let him go his way alone. This attitude never was universal nor was it consistently maintained, for there is hardly one of the older negroes who does not have a white man to whom he goes for advice or help in time of trouble — a sort of patron, in fact. Many a negro has been saved from the chain gang or the penitentiary because of such friendly interest, and many have been positively helped thereby toward good citizenship. Nevertheless there has been a tendency on the part of the whites to remain passive, to wait until the negro asked for help.

Undoubtedly there is now developing in the South a growing sense of responsibility for the welfare of the negro. The negro quarters of the towns, so long neglected, are receiving more attention from the street cleaners; better sidewalks are being built; and the streets are better lighted. The sanitary officers are more attentive. The landowner is building better cabins for his tenants and is encouraging them to plant gardens and to raise poultry and pigs. The labor contractor is providing better quarters, though conditions in many lumber and construction camps are still deplorable. Observant lawyers and judges say that they see an increasing number of cases in which juries evidently decide points of doubt in favor of negro defendants, even where white men are concerned. Socially minded citizens are forcing improvement of the disgraceful conditions which have often prevailed on chain gangs and in prisons. Nor

is this all.   More white men and women are teaching negroes than ever before.   The oldest university in the United States points proudly to the
number of Sunday schools for negroes conducted
by its students, and it is not alone in this high
endeavor.   Many Southern colleges and universities are studying the negro problem from all sides
and are trying to help in its solution.   The visiting
nurses in the towns spend a large proportion of
their time among the negroes, striving to teach
hygiene and sanitation.   White men frequently
lecture before negro schools.   Since the beginning
of the Great War negro women have been encouraged to aid in Red Cross work.   Negroes have
been appointed members of city or county committees of defense and have worked with the whites
in many branches of patriotic endeavor.   Negroes
have subscribed liberally in proportion to their
means for Liberty Bonds and War Savings Stamps
and have given liberally to war work.

The growth of a sense of responsibility for the
welfare of the negro upon the part of the more
thoughtful and more conscientious portion of the
white population has reduced racial friction in
many communities.   White women are evincing
more interest in the morals of black women than

was usual fifteen or twenty years ago. Ostracism is more likely to visit a white man who crosses the line. There is no means of knowing the actual amount of illicit intercourse, but the most competent observers believe it to be decreasing. Though the percentage of mulattoes has increased since 1890, according to the census, the figures are confessedly inaccurate, and the increase can be easily accounted for by the marriage of mulattoes with negroes, and the consequent diffusion of white blood. An aspiring negro is likely to seek a mulatto wife, and their children will be classed as mulattoes by the enumerators.

Except for the demagogues, whose abuse of the negro is their stock in trade, the most bitter denunciations come from those nearest to him in economic status. The town loafers, the cotton mill operatives, the small farmers, particularly the tenant farmers, are those who most frequently clash with both the impertinent and the self-respecting negro. In their eyes self-respect may not be differentiated from insolence. If a negro is not servile, they are likely to class him as impertinent or worse. The political success of Blease of South Carolina, Vardaman of Mississippi, and the late Jeff. Davis of Arkansas is largely due to their appeal to these types of whites. The negro on the other hand may resent the assumption of superiority on the part of men perhaps less efficient than himself. Obviously friction may arise under such conditions.

The mobs which have so often stained the reputation of the South by defiance of the law and by horrible cruelty as well do not represent the best elements of the South. The statement so often made that the most substantial citizens of a community compose lynching parties may have been partially true once, but it is not true today. These mobs are chiefly made up from the lowest third of the white community Perhaps the persistence of the belief has prevented the wiser part of the population from stamping out such lawlessness; perhaps some lingering feeling of mistaken loyalty to the white race restrains them from strong action; perhaps the individualism of the Southerner has interfered with general acceptance of the idea of the inexorable majesty of the law which must be vindicated at any cost. Yet, in spite of all these undercurrents of feeling, sheriffs and private citizens do on occasion brave the fury of enraged mobs to rescue or to protect. Attempts to prosecute participants in such mobs usually fail in the South as elsewhere, but occasionally a jury convicts.

The tradition that, years ago, lynching was only invoked in punishment of the unspeakable crime is more or less true. It is not true now. The statistics of lynching which are frequently presented are obviously exaggerated, as they include many cases which are simply the results of the sort of personal encounters which might and do occur anywhere. There is a tendency to class every case of homicide in which a negro is the victim as a lynching, which is manifestly unfair; but even though liberal allowance be made for this error, in the total of about 3000 cases tabulated in the last thirty years, the undisputed instances of mob violence are shamefully numerous. Rape is by no means the only crime thus punished; sometimes the charge is so trivial that one recoils in horror at the thought of taking human life as a punishment.

Yet it must not be forgotten that over certain parts of the South a nameless dread is always hovering. In some sections an unaccompanied white woman dislikes to walk through an unlighted village street at night; she hesitates to drive along a lonely country road in broad daylight without a pistol near her hand; and she does not dare to walk through the woods alone. The rural districts are poorly policed and the ears of the farmer working in the field are always alert for the sound of the bell or the horn calling for help, perhaps from his own home. Occasionally, in spite of all precautions some human animal, inflamed by brooding upon the unattainable, leaves a victim outraged and dead, or worse than dead. Granted that such a crime occurs in a district only once in ten, or even in twenty years; that is enough. Rural folks have long memories, and in the back of their minds persists an uncontrollable morbid dread. The news of another victim sometimes turns men into fiends who not only take life but even inflict torture beforehand. The mere suspicion of intent is sometimes enough to deprive such a community of its reason, for there are communities which have brooded over the possibility of the commission of the inexpiable crime until the residents are not quite sane upon this matter. Naturally calmness and forbearance in dealing with other and less heinous forms of negro crime are not always found in such a neighborhood. This fact helps to explain, though not to excuse, some of the riots that occur.

The better element in the South, however, opposes mob violence, and this opposition is growing stronger and more purposeful. Associations have

been formed to oppose mob rule and to punish participants. Where reputable citizens are lukewarm
it is largely because they have not realized that the
old tradition that lynching is the proper remedy for
rape cannot stand. If sudden, sharp retribution
were inflicted upon absolute proof, only for this one
cause, it is doubtful whether much effective opposition could be enlisted. Yet wiser men have seen
defiance of law fail to stop crime, have seen mobs
act upon suspicions afterward proved groundless,
have seen mob action widely extended, and have
seen the growth of a spirit of lawlessness. Where
one mob has had its way, another is always more
easily aroused, and soon the administration of the
law becomes a farce. In some years hardly a
third of the victims of this summary process have
been charged with rape or intent to commit rape.
As a consequence the sentiment that the law should
take its course in every case is steadily growing.[1]

Though mob fury has broken out on occasion in
every Southern State, Maryland, West Virginia,

_[1] The statistics on lynching do not always agree. Those compiled
at Tuskegee Institute list 38 cases for 1917 and 62 for 1918. The
National Association for the Advancement of Colored People in its
report *Thirty Years of Lynching* (1919) reports 67 cases for 1918, and
325 cases for the five-year period ending with 1918, of which 304 are
said to have occurred in the South.

Kentucky, and North Carolina are measurably free from such visitations. Over considerable periods of time, Georgia comes unenviably first, followed by Mississippi, Texas, and Louisiana. These four States have furnished a large majority of the lynchings. The other States range between the two groups, though in proportion to the negro element in its population Oklahoma has had a disproportionate share. It may be said that the lynchings occur chiefly in those sections or counties where the numbers of whites and negroes are nearly equal. They are fewer in the black belt and in those counties and States where whites are in an overwhelming majority.

No man has been wise enough to propose any solution of the negro question which does not require an immediate and radical change in human nature. As the proportion of negroes able to read and write grows larger, they will certainly demand full political rights, which the mass of the whites, so far as any one can judge, will be unwilling to allow. Deportation to Africa — proposed in all seriousness — is impossible. Negro babies are born faster than they could easily be carried away, even if there were no other obstacle. The suggestion that whites be expelled from a State or two, which would then be turned over to negroes, is likewise impracticable. Amalgamation apparently is going on more slowly now, and more rapid progress would presuppose a state of society and an attitude toward the negro entirely different from that which prevails anywhere in the United States. There is left then the theory that, with increasing wealth and wider diffusion of education, or even without them, the negro must take his place on equal terms in the American political and social system. This theory, of course, requires an absolute reversal of attitude upon the part of many millions of whites.

Color and race prejudice are stubborn things, and California and South Africa are no more free from such prejudices than the Southern States. In fact, South Africa is today wrestling with a problem much like that of the United States and is succeeding no better in solving it. The movement of negroes to the North and West, if continued on any large scale, seems likely to mean simply the diffusion of the problem and not its solution.

# CHAPTER VIII

## EDUCATIONAL PROGRESS

APOLOGISTS for Reconstruction have repeatedly asserted that the Reconstruction governments gave to the South a system of public schools unknown up to that time, with the implication that this boon more than compensated for the errors of those years. The statement has been so often made, and by some who should have known better, that it has generally been accepted at its face value. The status of public education in the South in 1860, it is true, was not satisfactory, and the percentage of illiteracy was high. Any attempt to distract attention from these facts by pointing out the great proportion of the Southern white population in colleges and academies is as much to be deprecated as the denial of the existence of public schools at all.[1]

[1] Some States had done little for public schools before 1860, but others had made more than a respectable beginning. Delaware established a "literary fund" in 1796, Tennessee in 1806, Virginia in

In general the public schools of the South began as charity schools, but this was also the case in several of the older States in other parts of the country. These schools were generally poorly taught in the early years, and it has been questioned whether the training which the pupils received compensated them for the humiliating acknowledgment of poverty which their attendance implied. The amount of money available was small, and the teacher was generally inefficient or worse, but these "old field schools" did help some men on their way. Several States went beyond the idea of charity in education, and some of the towns and cities established excellent schools for all the people.

The literary fund in North Carolina, for example, amounted to nearly $2,250,000 in 1840. The rapid increase of this fund had led to the establishment of public schools in 1839. To every district which raised $20 by local taxation, twice that amount was

1810, Maryland in 1813, and Georgia in 1817. Kentucky and Mississippi soon followed their example; North Carolina began to create such a fund in 1825; Alabama, Delaware, Georgia, Kentucky, Maryland, North Carolina, and South Carolina appropriated a part or the whole of their shares of the "surplus" distributed by the Federal Government under the Act of 1836 to increase these funds or establish new ones for the support of schools; and some States levied considerable taxes for the support of educational institutions.

given from the income of the literary fund. With
the election of Calvin H. Wiley as state superintendent of education in 1852, substantial progress
began. In 1860 there were over 3000 schools, and
the total expenditure was $279,000. The number
of illiterates had fallen proportionately and actually, and ten years more of uninterrupted work
would have done much to remove the stigma of
illiteracy. The school fund was left intact during
the Civil War, and most of the counties continued
to levy school taxes. A part of the fund was lost,
however, through the failure of the banks in which
it was invested, and the remainder was squandered
by the Reconstruction government. In spite of all
discouragements, Superintendent Wiley held on
until deposed by the provisional governor in 1865.
It is hardly an exaggeration to say that the schools
of this State were better in 1860 than they were
in 1880.

During the Reconstruction period a system of
schools was established in every one of the seceding
States. On paper these schemes were often admirable. Usually they were modeled after the system
in the State from which some influential carpet-
bagger came, and under normal conditions, if
honestly and judiciously administered, they would

have answered their ostensible purposes and would have done much to raise the intellectual level of the population. Conditions, however, were not normal. The production of wealth was hindered, and taxes had been increased to the point of confiscation. In States which had been ravaged by war, and of which the whole economic and social systems had been dislocated, an undue proportion of the total social income was demanded for the schools. Under existing conditions the communities could not support the schemes of education which had been projected. This fact is enough to account for their failure, for when an individual or a community is unable to pay the price demanded, it matters little how desirable or laudable the object may be.

As if to make failure doubly certain, the schools were neither honestly nor judiciously administered. Much money was deliberately stolen, and much more was wasted. Extravagant salaries were paid to favorites, and unnecessary equipment was bought at exorbitant prices. The authorities in several States seemed more interested in the idea of educating negro children with white children than in the real process of education. Though in but four States — South Carolina, Mississippi, Louisiana, and Arkansas — were mixed schools the only schools, such an arrangement was understood to be the ultimate goal in several other States. Several of the state superintendents were negroes, and others were carpetbaggers dependent upon negro votes. Before the end of Reconstruction, several of these were forced to flee to avoid arrest for malfeasance in office. In those States where mixed schools alone were provided, white children did not attend and were thus cut off from educational opportunities at public expense. Where separate schools were provided, the teachers were often carpetbaggers who strove "to make treason odious." It is hardly surprising that some parents objected to having their children forced to sing *John Brown's Body* and to yield assent to the proposition that all Southerners were barbarians and traitors who deserved hanging.

Just after the close of the Civil War, thousands of white women went South to teach in schools which were established for negroes by Northern churches or benevolent associations. Every one who reads the reports of such organizations now, fifty years after, must be touched by the lofty faith and the burning zeal which impelled many of these educational missionaries; but he must also

11

be astonished by their ignorance of the negro and their blindness to actual conditions. They went with an ideal negro in their minds, and at first, they treated the negro as though he were their ideal of what a negro ought to be. The phases through which the majority of these teachers went were enthusiasm, doubt, disillusionment, and despair. Some left the South and their charges, holding that conditions were to blame rather than their methods; but others were clearsighted enough to realize that they had set about solving the problem in the wrong way.

Beginning with the assumption that the negro was equal or superior to the white in natural endowment and burning with resentment against his "oppressors," they attempted to bridge the gap of centuries in a generation. They were anxious to bring the negro into contact with the culture of the white race and thereby they strengthened the conclusion to which the negro had already jumped that educational and manual labor were an impossible combination. Then, too, in order to prove the sincerity of their belief in the brotherhood of mankind, they entered into the most intimate association with their pupils and their families. Some of them, we know, were compelled to struggle hard to overcome their instinctive repugnance to such intimacy. All of them taught by implication, and some by precept as well, that the Southern whites who held themselves apart were enemies to the blacks. That these teachers did some good is undoubted, but whether in the end a true balance would show more good than harm is not so certain.

When the native whites resumed control after the days of Reconstruction, their first thought was to reduce the expenses of the State. Tax levies were cut to the bone, school taxes among them. The school funds did not always suffer proportionately, however. In 1870, when the whites secured control in North Carolina, the expenditure for public schools in that State was $152,000. In 1874, the school revenue was over $412,000, and the number of white pupils was almost the same as in 1860; in addition 55,000 negroes were receiving instruction, but the school term was only ten weeks. The negro seems to have received in the first years of the new régime a fair share of the school money, but that share was not large. The reaction from Reconstruction extravagance was long-continued, and perhaps has not disappeared today.

Though the South was unable properly to support

one efficient system, it now attempted to maintain two, one for whites and the other for blacks.
Necessarily both systems were inadequate. The
usual country school was only a rude frame or
log building, sometimes without glass windows, in
which one untrained teacher, without apparatus or
the simplest conveniences, attempted to give instruction in at least half a dozen subjects to a group
of children of all ages during a period of ten to fifteen weeks a year. Often even this meager period
was divided into a summer and winter term, on the
plea that the older children could not be spared
from the farms for the whole time or that bad roads
and stormy weather prevented the youngest from
attending during the winter.

Though it seems almost incredible under such
conditions, something was nevertheless accomplished. Many children, it is true, learned little or
nothing and gave up the pretense of attending
school. Others, however, found something to feed
their hungry minds and, when they had exhausted
what their neighborhood school had to offer, they
attended the academies which had been reëstab-
lished or had sprung up in the villages nearby or
at the countyseat. Between 1875 and 1890, it was
not at all uncommon to find in such academies

grown men and women studying the regular high school subjects. Some had previously taught rural schools and now sought further instruction; and others had worked on the farms or had been in business. Men of twenty-five or thirty sat in classes with town children of fifteen or sixteen, but made such a large proportion of the total attendance that they did not feel embarrassed by the contrast in ages.

In the eighties there were scores of these academies, institutes, and seminaries in the towns of the South. They were not well graded; the teachers may never have heard of pedagogy. Their libraries were small or altogether lacking, and their apparatus was scanty; but in spite of these drawbacks an unusually large proportion of the students were desirous to learn. Many teachers loved mathematics or Latin, and some of the students gained a thorough if narrow preparation for college. An examination of college registers of the period shows a considerable proportion of students of twenty-five or thirty years of age. There is even a case where a college student remained out a term in order to attend a session of the Legislature to which he had been elected. The college students of the late seventies and early eighties were serious minded and thought of questions as men and not as boys. Though the clapper of the college bell was sometimes thrown into the well or the president's wagon was transferred to the chapel roof, these things were often done from a sort of sense of duty: college students were expected to be mischievous. Yet the whole tone of college life was serious. There were no organized college athletics, no musical or dramatic clubs, no other outside activities such as those to which the student of to-day devotes so much of his attention, except, of course, the "literary societies" for practice in declamation and debating.

Though many towns established graded schools before 1890 by means of special taxes, the condition of rural education at this time was disheartening. The percentage of negro illiteracy was falling, because it could not easily be raised, but the reduction of white illiteracy was slow. The school terms were still short, and many of the school buildings were unfit for human occupation. On the other hand, the quality of the teachers was improving. The short term of the schools was being lengthened by private subscription in some districts, and new and adequate buildings appeared in others. Progress was evidently being made, even if it was not obtrusive, and in that progress one of the leading factors was the Peabody Fund.

In 1867 George Peabody, a native of Massachusetts but then a banker of London, who had laid the foundation of his fortune in Baltimore, placed in the hands of trustees $2,100,000 in securities to be used for the encouragement of education in the Southern States. The Fund was increased to $3,500,000 in 1869, though a considerable part consisted of bonds of Mississippi and Florida which those States refused to recognize as valid obligations. The chairman of the trustees for many years was Robert C. Winthrop of Massachusetts, and the other members of the board were distinguished men, both Northern and Southern. The first general agent, as the active administrator was called, was Barnas Sears, who at the time of his election was president of Brown University.

Dr. Sears was an unusual man, who comprehended conditions in the South and was disposed to improve them in every feasible way by using the resources at his command. He had no inflexible program and was willing to modify his plans to fit changing conditions. The income of the Fund appears small in this day of munificent foundations, but it seemed large then; and its effects were far-reaching. Sears was not an educational reformer in the modern sense. He seems to have had no new philosophy of education but took the best schools of the nation as a standard and strove to bring the schools of the South up to that standard. Through the aid of the Fund model schools were established in every State. The University of North Carolina opened its doors to the teachers of the State for professional training during the summer and was apparently the first of the summer schools now so numerous and popular. Direct appropriations in aid of schools were made out of the Fund, provided the community by taxation or subscription raised much larger sums. The Peabody Normal College at Nashville, Tennessee, was founded, and no effort was spared to develop a general interest in public education. Advice to legislatures, trustees, or communities was given when asked but so tactfully that neither resentment nor suspicion was aroused.

Before his death, Dr. Sears had chosen Dr. J. L. M. Curry as his successor, and the choice was promptly ratified by the trustees. Dr. Curry was a thorough Southerner, a veteran of both the Mexican and the Civil War. He had first practiced law and had sat in the House of Representatives of the

United States and of the Confederate States.  At the time of his election to the management of the Peabody Fund he was a professor in Richmond College, Virginia, and a minister of the Baptist Church.  He had a magnetic personality, an unyielding belief in the value of education for both white and black, and the temperament and gifts of the orator.  As a Southerner, he could speak more freely and more effectively to the people than his predecessor, who had done the pioneer work. During the years of his service, Curry therefore gave himself chiefly to the development of public sentiment, making speeches at every opportunity before societies, conventions, and other gatherings. As he himself said, he addressed legislatures "from the Potomac to the Rio Grande."

While the influence of the Peabody Fund and its agents was large, it was not the only influence upon the educational development of the South.   There were throughout that section men who saw clearly that the main hope centered in education for black and white.   They talked in season and out, though sometimes with little apparent result, for the opposing forces were strong.  Among these forces poverty was perhaps the strongest.   It is difficult to convince a people who must struggle for the bare necessities of life that taxation for any purpose is a positive good; and a large proportion of the families of the rural South handled little money. This was true even for years after the towns began to feel the thrill of growing industrialism. It has sometimes seemed that the poorer a man and the larger the number of his children, the greater his dread of taxes for education.

Then, too, the Southern people had followed the tradition of Jefferson that the best government is that which assumes the fewest functions and interferes least with the individual. Many honest men who meant to be good citizens felt that education belonged to the family or the church and could not see why the State should pay for teaching any more than for preaching, or for food, or clothing, or shelter. There were, of course, those claiming to hold this theory whose underlying motives were selfish. They had property which they had inherited or accumulated, and they objected to paying taxes for educating other people's children. It must be said, however, that as a class, the larger taxpayers have been more ready to vote higher taxes for schools than the poor and illiterate, whose morbid dread of taxation has been fostered by the politician.

There were others who were cold to the extension of public education on account of the schools already existing. In many towns and villages there were struggling academies, often nominally under church auspices. Towns which could have supported one school were trying to support two or three. In few cases was any direct financial aid given by the religious organization, but the school was known as the Methodist or the Presbyterian school, because the teaching force and the majority of the patrons belonged to that denomination. The denominational influence behind these schools was often lukewarm toward the extension of public education, and the ministers themselves had been known to make slighting references to "godless schools." There was still another class of people who really opposed public schools because they did not believe that the masses should be educated. This class was, however, small and is perhaps more numerous in other sections of the Union than in the South.

Last, but by no means the least, of the obstacles to general public education was the question of its influence upon the negro. The apparent effects of negro education were not likely to make the average white man feel that the experiment had been successful.   The phrase that "an educated negro was a good plough-hand spoiled" seemed to meet with general acceptance.   The smattering of an education which the negroes had received — it would be difficult to call it more — seemed to have improved neither their efficiency nor their morals. As a result there were many white people so short-sighted that they would starve their own children rather than feed the negro.

To all of these obstacles in human nature were added the defects of the tax system.   Almost invariably the tax was levied by the Legislature upon the State as a whole or upon the county, and the constitutions or the laws in some cases forbade the progressive smaller division to levy special taxes for any purpose.   Graded schools began, however, to appear in the incorporated towns which were not subject to the same tax limitations as the rural districts, and in time it became easier to levy supplementary local taxes by legislative act, judicial interpretation, or constitutional changes.

Gradually public sentiment in favor of schools grew stronger.   The legislatures raised the rate of taxation for school purposes, normal schools were established, log schoolhouses began to be replaced by frame or brick structures, uniform textbooks became the rule and not the exception, teachers' salaries were raised, and the percentage of attendance climbed upward, though there was still a remnant of the population which did not attend at all. The school term was not proportionately extended, since a positive mania for small districts developed — a school at every man's door.   In the olden days large districts were common, and many of the children walked four or five miles to school in the morning and back home in the afternoon.   No one then dreamed of transporting the children at public expense.   The school authorities were often unable to resist the pressure to make new districts, and necessarily a contracted term followed.   In 1900 the average school term in North Carolina was not longer than in 1860, though much more money was spent, and the salaries were little higher.   It must be remembered, of course, that no appropriations were made for negro education before the Civil War.

Both during and after the War many schools were opened for negroes by Freedmen's Aid Societies, various philanthropic associations, and denominational boards or committees.   As public schools were established for negroes, some of these organizations curtailed their work and others withdrew altogether. Others persisted, however, and new schools have been founded by these and similar organizations, by private philanthropy, and also by negro churches. As a result there are independent schools, state schools, and Federal schools. The recent monumental report of the Bureau of Education reports 653 schools for negroes other than regular public schools.[1] Of these 28 are under public control, 507 are denominational schools (of which 354 are under white boards and 153 under negro boards), and 118 are classed as independent. This last group includes not only the great national schools, such as Tuskegee and Hampton, but small private enterprises supported chiefly by irregular donations. These private and independent schools owned property valued at $28,496,946 and had an income of over $3,000,000. State and Federal appropriations at the date of the report reached about $963,000.

During the first years after the downfall of the Reconstruction governments the negro received a fair proportion of the pittance devoted to public schools. Governor Vance of North Carolina, in recommending in 1877 an appropriation to the

[1] *Negro Education*, Bureau of Education Bulletins 38 and 39 (1916). This work supersedes all previous collections of facts upon negro education.

University for a "professorship for the purpose of instructing in the theory and art of teaching" went on to state that "a school of similar character should be established for the education of colored teachers, the want of which is more deeply felt by the black race even than the white. . . . Their desire for education is a very creditable one, and should be gratified so far as our means will permit." Instead of establishing the chair of pedagogy recommended by Governor Vance, the Legislature appropriated the money to conduct the summer school for teachers at the University. An appropriation of equal amount was made for negroes and similar allowances have been continued to the present. Proportionately larger appropriations have been made for the whites in recent years. Other States have established normal schools for negroes, but in none of them is the supply of trained negro teachers equal to the demand.

The negro public schools were organized along the same lines as the white, so far as circumstances permitted, but the work was difficult and remains so to this day. The negro teachers were ignorant, and many of them were indolent and immoral. In only a few places in the South do whites teach negroes in public schools. The enthusiasm for education displayed just after emancipation gradually wore off, and many parents showed little interest in the education of their children. Education had not proved the "open sesame" to affluence, and many parents were unwilling or unable to compel their children to attend school. As a contributory cause of this reluctance the poverty of the negro must be considered. It was difficult for the negro to send to school a child who might be of financial aid to the family. To many negro parents it seemed a matter of little moment to keep a child away from school one or two days a week to assist at home. It must also be remembered that the negro tenant farmer is migratory in his habits and that he often moved in the middle of the short term. Consequently the whole value of the term might easily be lost by the transfer. It is not surprising that the final product of such unstable educational conditions was not impressive.

The idea of the first educational missionaries to the negroes of the South was to turn them into white men as soon as possible by bringing them into contact with the traditional culture of the whites through the study of Latin, Greek, mathematics, and sometimes Hebrew, especially in the case of students for the ministry. The attempt was made to take the negro, fresh from slavery and with no cultural background, through the course generally pursued by whites. Numerous "universities" and "colleges" were founded with this end in view. Hampton Institute with its insistence upon fitting education to the needs of the race was unique for a time, though later it received the powerful support of Tuskegee Institute and its noted principal and founder, Booker T. Washington. The influence of this educational prophet was great in the North, whence came most of the donations for private schools. In imitation many mushroom schools have recently added "rural" or "industrial" to their names, but few of them are doing work of great value. Where the school appeals chiefly to the negro for support, liberal use is made of such high-sounding names as "college" and "university." The negro still thinks that the purpose of education is to free him from manual labor, and he looks with little favor upon a school which requires actual industrial training. For the same reason he is quick to protest when the attempt is made to introduce manual training into the public schools.

Partly because of this opposition on the part of the negroes themselves, partly because industrial training is more expensive than purely academic

12

training, and partly because such training has only recently been recognized as part of education, the South has made little provision for the industrial education of the negro at public expense. According to the *Report on Negro Education*, few of the agricultural and mechanical schools maintained partly by the Federal land grants and partly by the States are really efficient. A few state or city schools also give manual training. About one-third of the private schools for negroes offer industrial courses, but much of this work is ineffective — either so slight as to be negligible or straight labor done in return for board and tuition and without regard to educational value. Hampton and Tuskegee are known to do excellent work, and a few of the smaller schools are to be classed as efficient; but in the great majority of negro schools the old curriculum is still followed, and the students gladly submit to its exactness. Why study something so plebeian as carpentry when one may study such scholarly subjects as Latin or Greek?

Most institutions for negroes desire to do work of college grade. Some with not a single pupil above the elementary grades nevertheless proudly call themselves colleges. Other so-called colleges have secondary pupils but none in college classes.

Thirty-three institutions do have a total of 1643 students in college classes and 994 students in professional courses, but these same schools enroll more than 10,000 pupils in elementary and secondary grades. Some of them are attempting to maintain college classes for less than 5 per cent of their enrollment, and the teaching force gives a disproportionate share of time to such students. Two of these thirty-three institutions have nearly all the professional students, and two have nearly half the total number of college students. Only three can properly be called colleges — Howard University at Washington, Fisk University, and Meharry Medical College at Nashville, Tennessee.

While several of the Southern States have greatly increased their expenditures for schools since 1910, in some cases more than doubling them, the proportion devoted to negro schools has not been greatly increased, if indeed it has been increased at all. For example, in North Carolina, which assigns for negro education much more than the average of the States containing any considerable proportion of negroes, the total paid to negro teachers in 1910–11 was $340,856, as against $1,715,994 paid to white teachers. Five years later, negro teachers received $536,272, but white teachers received $3,258,352. In other words, in the former year all the negro teachers received one-fifth as much as all the whites, while five years later they received about one-sixth; that is, something less than one-third the total number of children received about one-seventh of the money expended for instruction. A part of this wide difference in expenditure may be explained or even defended. The districts or townships which have voted additional local taxes are usually those in which there are comparatively few negroes. The average salary paid to negro teachers, although low, is as large as can be earned in most of the occupations open to them, and any sudden or large increase would neither immediately raise the standard of competency nor insure a much larger proportion of the ability of the race. The percentage of school attendance of negro children is lower than in the case of white children. Very few negro children, whether because of economic pressure, lack of ability, or lack of desire for knowledge, complete even the fifth grade. Among negroes there is little real demand for high school instruction, which is more expensive than elementary instruction. Therefore, the proportion of the total funds spent for negro education might properly be less than their numbers would indicate. If the proportionate amount spent today for the instruction of certain racial groups of the foreign population could be separated from the total, it would be found that less than the average is spent upon them for the same reasons. However, when all allowances have been made, it is obvious that the negro is receiving less than a fair share of the appropriations made by the Southern States for education.

The inadequate public schools for negroes have been excused or justified upon the ground that private and church schools are supplying the need. This is true in some localities, for the great majority of negro private schools, no matter by what name they are called, are really doing only elementary or secondary work. These schools, however, only touch the beginnings of the problem and have served in some degree to lessen the sense of responsibility for negro education on the part of the Southern whites. Where there is one of these schools supported by outside philanthropy, the public school is likely to be less adequately equipped and supported than in the towns where no such school exists. But at best, these schools can reach only a small proportion of the children.

The difficulty lies in public sentiment. As a rule

the tax rate is fixed by the State but collected by the county, and the county board divides the amount plus any local taxes levied, among the schools. Districts of the same number of pupils may receive widely varying amounts, according to the grade of instruction demanded. Generally, a part of the fund is apportioned per capita, and the remainder is divided according to the supposed special need of the districts. A white district which demands high grade teachers is given the necessary money, if possible. Few colored schools have advanced pupils, and only sufficient funds for a cheaper teacher or teachers may be provided. Colored districts are often made too large. The white districts ask so much that little more than the per capita appropriation is left for the colored schools. The negroes are politically powerless and public sentiment does not demand that money be taken from white children to be given to negroes.

Mention should be made of several funds which have been established by philanthropists for the education of the negro. The John F. Slater Fund, founded by a gift of $1,000,000 in 1882, has now reached $1,750,000. The greater part of the income is devoted to the encouragement of training schools. No schools are established by the Fund itself, but it coöperates with the local authorities and the General Education Board. The Jeanes Fund of $1,000,000 established by a Quaker lady, Miss Anna T. Jeanes of Philadelphia, expends the greater part of its income in helping to pay the salaries of county supervisors for rural schools. These are usually young colored women, who work under the direction of the county superintendents and visit the rural schools. They give simple talks upon hygiene and sanitation, encourage better care of schoolhouses and grounds, stimulate interest in gardening and simple home industries, and encourage self help. Their work has been exceedingly valuable. The Phelps Stokes Fund of $900,-000, founded by Miss Caroline Phelps Stokes, is not wholly devoted to the negroes of the South. It has been expended chiefly in the study of the negro problem, in founding fellowships, and in making possible the valuable report on negro education already mentioned. In 1914, Mr. Julius Rosenwald of Chicago offered to every negro rural community wishing to erect a comfortable and adequate school building a sum not to exceed $300, provided that the community would obtain from private or public funds at least as much more.

The interest of the General Education Board is

not limited either to negro or even to Southern education, but it has done much for both. This great foundation has paid salaries of state supervisors of negro schools in several States and has coöperated with the Jeanes Fund in maintaining county supervisors of negro schools. It has appropriated over half a million dollars to industrial schools and about one-fourth as much to negro colleges. Farm demonstration work, of which more is said elsewhere, is also of aid to the negroes. The Board has realized, however, that the development of negro schools is dependent upon the economic and educational progress of the whites, and has contributed most to white schools or to objects of a nature intended to benefit the whole population.

All testimony points to the conclusion that there is now real enthusiasm for education among the Southern whites. The school terms are being extended, often by means of local taxes levied in addition to the minimum fixed by the State; the quality of the teaching is improving; and popular interest is growing. In many sections, the school is developing into a real community center. Good buildings are replacing the shacks formerly so common. North Carolina is proud of the fact that for more than fourteen years an average of more than one new school a day has been built from plans approved by the educational department. More and more attention is being paid to the surroundings of the buildings. School gardens are common, and some schools even cultivate an acre or two of ground, the proceeds of which go to furnish apparatus or supplies. Many of the Southern towns and cities have schools which need not fear comparison with those in other sections.

The crying need is more money which can come only in two ways, by reforming the system of taxation, and by increasing the amount of taxable property. All through the South the chief reliance is a general property tax with local assessors who are either incompetent or else desirous of keeping down assessments. The proportion of assessment to value varies widely, but on the average it can hardly be more than fifty per cent; and, as invariably happens, the assessment of the more valuable properties is proportionately less than that of the small farm or the mechanic's home. The South is growing richer, but the conflict with the North set the section back thirty or forty years, while the remainder of the country was increasing in wealth. Even today the South must build two school systems without the aid of government land grants, which have had so much to do with the successful development of the schools of the Western States, and without the commercial prosperity which has come to the East. The rate of taxation levied for schools in many Southern communities is now among the highest in the United States.

During the past ten years, hundreds of public high schools have been established, more than half of which are rural. Some still follow the old curriculum, but a new institution known as the "farm life school" is now being developed. Many other schools have such a department attached and usually give instruction in household economics as well. The General Education Board estimates that $20,000,000 has been spent for improved buildings since the appointment of professors of secondary education in Southern universities. This, by the way, is one of the most useful contributions of the Board. These men, chosen by the institutions themselves as regular members of the faculty but with their salaries paid by an appropriation from the Board, may give a course or two in the university, but their chief duties are to coordinate the work of the high schools and to serve as educational missionaries. They go up and down the States, exhorting, advising, and stimulating the people, and the fruits of their work are present on every hand.

The South has a superabundance of colleges. Some of them have honorable records; others represent faith and hope or denominational zeal rather than accomplishment. Some of the older institutions were kept open during War and Reconstruction but others were forced to close. With the return of white supremacy old institutions have been revived and new ones have been founded. The number of students has increased, but the financial difficulties of the institutions have hardly diminished. Few had any endowment worth considering, and the so-called state institutions received very small appropriations or none at all. Good preparatory schools were few and, since the colleges were dependent upon tuition fees, many students with inadequate preparation were leniently admitted. Preparatory departments were established for those students who could not possibly be admitted to college classes. Necessarily the quality of work was low, though many institutions struggled for the maintenance of respectable standards. One college president frankly said: "We are liberal about letting young men into the Freshman class, but particular about letting them out."

It was not uncommon for half of a first year class to be found deficient and turned back at the end of the year, or dismissed as hopeless. Obviously this was a wasteful method of determining competency.

Vanderbilt University at Nashville, Tennessee, founded in 1873 by the gifts of "Commodore" Vanderbilt, was the first Southern institution with anything approaching an adequate endowment and was the first to insist upon thorough preparation for entrance, though it was compelled to organize a sub-freshman class in the beginning. Its policy had considerable influence both upon college standards and upon the growth of private preparatory schools. The development of public schools, for a time, had made the work of colleges in general more difficult, because they supplanted scores of private academies which had done passably well the work of college preparation and yet were not themselves able to prepare students for college in the first years of their existence. For years it was difficult in many localities for a young man to secure proper preparation, and the total of poorly prepared students applying for admission to the colleges increased. The number of towns and cities which have established high schools or high school departments has since increased rapidly, and today a larger and larger proportion of college students comes from public schools.

Since 1900, the resources of the colleges have greatly increased. States which appropriated a few thousand dollars for higher education in the early nineties now appropriate ten or even twenty times as much to their universities, agricultural colleges, and normal and technical schools for women, and have appropriated millions for new buildings. Many of the denominational colleges have obtained substantial endowments. The General Education Board up to 1914 had subscribed over $3,000,000 to Southern colleges and universities on condition that the institutions raise at least three times as much more. Southern men who have accumulated wealth are realizing their social responsibility. Several recent gifts of a million dollars or more are not included in the sum mentioned above, and many smaller gifts or bequests likewise.

Standards of work have been raised with increasing income. As elsewhere the effect of the reports of the Carnegie Foundation has been patent. The stronger institutions have brought up their requirements to the minimum, on paper at least, and to a great extent in fact. Some of the weaker institutions have dropped the pretense of doing college work; others have accepted the position of junior colleges doing two years of college work and giving no degrees. The States exercise little or no supervision over the quality of work done for college degrees, and some institutions continue to grant diplomas for what is really secondary work, but the fact that they are not up to the standard is known and the management is generally apologetic.

No other phase of Southern life is more hopeful and more encouraging than the educational revival. True, judged by the standards of the richer States, the terms of the rural schools are short and the pay of the teachers is small; but both are being increased, and no schools are exercising more wholesome influence. The high schools are neither so numerous nor so well equipped as in some other States, but nowhere else is such evident progress being made. There are no universities in the South which count their income in millions, but the number of institutions adequately equipped to do efficient work is already large and increasing. The spirit of faculty and students is admirable, and the contact of the institutions and the people of the Southern States is increasingly close and full of promise.

# CHAPTER IX

## THE SOUTH OF TODAY

THE South of the present is a changing South with its face toward the future rather than the past. Nevertheless the dead hand is felt by all the people a part of the time, and some of the people are never free from its paralyzing touch. Old prejudices, the remembrance of past grievances, and antipathies long cherished now and then assert themselves in the most unexpected fashion. The Southerner, no matter how much he may pride himself upon being liberal and broad, is likely to make certain reservations and limitations in his attitude. There are some questions upon which he is not open to argument, certain subjects which he cannot discuss freely and dispassionately. Some Southerners have so many of these reservations that conversation with them is difficult unless one instinctively understands their psychology and is willing to avoid certain subjects. The past has made so powerful an impression upon them that it has affected their whole attitude of mind.

Time, travel, association, engrossing work, and economic prosperity have weakened many of these prejudices and antipathies, however, and the Southerner is becoming free.    There are individuals who will always be bound by the past; there are some men, and more women, who are yet "unreconstructed"; there are neighborhoods and villages where men and women yet live in the past and absolutely refuse to attempt to adjust themselves cheerfully to changed and changing conditions. This is not true of the Southern people as a whole. In fact there is danger that the younger generation will think too little of the past.    Much of the Old South is worthy of preservation, and it is never safe for a country or a section to break too abruptly with its older life.

Economically the South has prospered in proportion as the new spirit has ruled.    The question of secession is dead, and the man who refuses today to treat it as past history but grows excited in discussing it is not likely to be successful in his business or profession.    The men of the New South spend little time in discussing the relative wisdom of Jefferson Davis and Robert Toombs or the reasons for the failure of the Confederacy. The Southerners accept the results of the War, and all except a negligible minority are convinced that the preservation of the Union was for the best. To be sure they believe, partly through knowledge but more largely through absorption, that the Confederate soldier was the best fighting man ever known and that the War might have been won if the civil government had been wiser, but on the whole they are not sorry that secession failed. They thrill even today to *Dixie*, and *The Bonnie Blue Flag*, but this feeling is now purely emotional.

All the Southern States have felt, though unequally, the effects of industrialism. The South Atlantic States have been most influenced by this movement, but even Mississippi and Arkansas have been affected. In many sections the traveler is seldom out of sight of the factory chimney. Some towns, in appearance and spirit, might easily seem to belong to a Middle Western environment but for the presence of the negro and the absence of the foreign born. The population in these Southern towns is still overwhelmingly American. In no States except Maryland and Texas did the foreign born number as many as 100,000 in 1910, and Mississippi, North Carolina, and South Carolina each

13

had less than 10,000 at that time. The highest percentage of foreign born was 8.6 per cent in Delaware, the lowest 0.3 per cent in North Carolina. In the South as a whole the proportion of foreign born whites was only 2.5 per cent.

The laborers in the Southern shops and mills to-day are not only native born but almost altogether Southern born. The South has been a great loser through interstate migration. Other sections also have lost but the excess of those departing has been replaced by the immigration of foreign born. Comparatively few have come to the South from other sections except in Florida, Arkansas, Oklahoma, and Texas, and fewer foreign born have settled in the South. As a result, the percentage of increase of population is less for the South, if Oklahoma be omitted, than for the United States as a whole. Many of the laborers are of rural origin or are only a generation removed from the farm. They preserve the individualistic attitude of the rural mind and have learned little of collective action. Labor unions have made small progress except in a few skilled trades and class consciousness has not developed in the South.

The important industries have thus far been few and they have kept rather close to the original raw material.  The South does not spin all the cotton it produces, does not weave all the yarn it spins, and does not manufacture into clothing any considerable quantity of the cloth it weaves.  The greater part of both yarn and cloth is coarse, though some mills do finer work.  Little bleaching or printing, however, is done.  The South is a land of curious economic contrasts.  It produces sugar but buys confectionery.  It produces immense quantities of lumber but works up comparatively little, and this mainly into simple forms.  It produces iron and steel in considerable quantities but has few machine shops where really delicate work can be done.  It does not manufacture motor cars, electric or even textile machinery or machine tools, nor does it make watches or firearms in appreciable quantities.  In short, the South carries some of the most important raw materials only a step or two toward their ultimate form and depends upon other parts of the country for the finished article.

Years ago the story was told of a Georgia funeral at which that State furnished only the corpse and the grave.  Georgia, and other States too, can do much more today, if the funeral be not too elaborate.  It can furnish a cotton shroud, each year of finer quality.  The knitting mills of the South are able to supply an increasing proportion of the population with hose and underclothing, and a number of the mills are gaining a national trade through advertising. If demanded, Southern-made shoes may be found, and a Southern-made coffin may be drawn on a Southern-made wagon by Southern-bred horses and perhaps, though improbably, in harness of local manufacture also.

The South was once the richest section of the Union. The vicissitudes of the Civil War rendered it poor, but now it is rapidly growing richer and since the beginning of the Great War has shown a phenomenal accumulation of new capital. During this great struggle some of the cotton mills made in a single month profits as large as they were formerly accustomed to make in a year. Even though the farmer received for his cotton much more than usual, the price of cloth would still have yielded a profit to the manufacturer if cotton had been twice as high. Other enterprises have likewise been profitable, and when normal conditions are restored this capital will seek new investment. While prophecy is dangerous it seems probable that manufacturing in the South will grow as never before; and new forms of investment must be found, as the rural districts cannot furnish any

greatly increased supply of labor for cotton manufacturing though the towns can supply some adult
labor for other forms of industry.

The labor question is beginning to grow serious
in some localities, though it is difficult to discover
whether the problem is chiefly one of getting labor
at all or of getting it at something like the wages
formerly paid.   Apparently, however, the industrial growth of the South has been more rapid than
that of population.   Heretofore the farmer has had
little difficulty in obtaining some sort of assistance in cultivating his land, and this abundance of
labor has lessened the demand for agricultural machinery.   Now the migration of the negro to the
North has created a shortage of labor which must
force the farmer to purchase machinery.   Too
much man and horse power has been employed
upon Southern farms in proportion to the results
achieved.   The South has been producing a large
value per acre but a small value per individual.
If the South is to become permanently prosperous,
fewer persons must do the work and must even
increase the production.

A practical cotton-picking machine would help
to solve some of the South's problems, as any
family can plant and cultivate after a fashion

much more cotton than it can pick. Many attempts to produce such a machine have been made, but simplicity, efficiency, and cheapness have not yet been attained. Like the reaper and binder, a machine of this sort is needed for only a small portion of the year, but in that short period the need is extreme. Such a machine would revolutionize the tenant system, would permit a larger production of food, and at the same time would set labor free for other occupations. Meanwhile the general rate of wages in agriculture has risen and must rise still further, as it has done in other occupations. Any student of economics who draws his conclusions from observation of life as well as from books realizes how large a part custom plays in determining wages, and hitherto farm wages have been very low and labor has been inefficient in the South.

The economic future of the South must rest upon the advance of the farmer. This thesis has already been developed at length in another chapter, where the present unsatisfactory organization and conditions of agriculture were also discussed. Improvement, however, is already becoming evident. Cotton furnishes two-fifths of the value of all farm products, with corn, hay, tobacco, and wheat following in the order named. Gradually the West is ceasing to be the granary and the smokehouse of the Southern farmer, but the South does not yet feed itself. In 1917 only Maryland, Delaware, Virginia, and Oklahoma produced a surplus of wheat, though it is estimated that the South as a whole reduced its deficiency by more than 35,000,-000 bushels. The abnormal prices of agricultural products since 1915 have brought many farmers out of debt and set them on the road toward prosperity, but many have not yet realized that they are no longer objects of commiseration. Though the high prices of war times have brought prosperity to the farmer, the crying necessity today is a larger production per man employed.

The political, as well as the economic, condition of the South today is full of interest. Politically the common man is in control, and as a rule he selects men of his own type to represent him. The primary was almost universal in the South when the West was only thinking of it as a radical innovation. The day of aristocratic domination is over, if indeed it ever really existed. In many instances descent from well-known ancestors who have held high positions has proved a positive detriment to a political candidate of today. Some of the successful politicians, as might be expected, are demagogues. States differ in the number of politicians of this type, and the same State may vary from year to year. It may at the same time send a demagogue and a statesman to the Senate. Men are permitted to hold offices, both national and state, for longer periods than formerly, and, as a result, in recent Democratic Congresses Southern men have held the most important chairmanships.[1]

That the Southern representation in Congress is equal in ability, culture, and character to that of the Old South or to that of even thirty years ago can hardly be seriously maintained. There are in Congress a few men today who recall the best traditions of Southern leadership; there are more who are mediocre and parochial. For the most part they come from law offices in country towns, and have the virtues and the limitations of their environment. They are honest financially, if not intellectually, and do not consciously yield to "the interests." They are correct in their private lives and likely to be somewhat bigoted. Many are convinced that cities are essentially wicked and

[1] North Carolina, for example, had in the 65th Congress, the chairmanship of the Committees on Finance and on Rules in the Senate, and on Ways and Means, Rules, Judiciary, and Rivers and Harbors in the House, besides other chairmanships of less account. Seldom in the whole history of the country has the representation of any State been so powerful.

conceive them to be inhabited by vampires and parasites. Few can think in national terms, and fewer have either knowledge or comprehension of international relations. For a generation the South was excluded from any real participation in national affairs and was wholly occupied with local questions. It is therefore difficult for such men to realize the present position of the United States in world politics. With much perturbation of spirit the rank and file followed the President in the steps leading up to the Great War, though some of the would-be leaders attempted to rebel. On the other hand, some of the most valuable men in the great crisis were Southerners.

The dominant party in the South is called Democratic, but the name has little of its original significance today. The representative is likely to follow the sentiment of his district if he can discover it. Some of the Southern Democrats advocate doctrines which are far removed from traditional democracy, for Populistic ideas have not entirely died out and some of the farmers still demand special privileges, which, however, they would be the first to deny to any one else. Democracy in the South really means the white man's party, and the Democratic doctrines are those in which it is thought the majority of the white men of the State or section believe for the time.   Though the negro is no longer a voting power, the malign influence of the negro question persists.

Since the South as a whole favors prohibition of the liquor traffic the representatives of the people are almost unanimously in favor of prohibition, forgetting all constitutional scruples and all questions of state rights.   The sentiment for woman suffrage is not yet overwhelming and consequently, as might be surmised, conscientious scruples prevent representatives from voting for the extension of the franchise.   In two States, however, the friends of woman suffrage, though not strong enough to pass a constitutional amendment, have realized their aim by a brilliant *coup*.   Since most elections are practically settled in the primaries, the legislatures of Texas and Arkansas gave women the right to vote in such elections.   In other words, women were given the right to help nominate candidates, though they are excluded from the formal elections.   Whether these acts will stand in the courts has not been determined.   Missouri and Tennessee have recently given national suffrage to women, and Oklahoma has given full suffrage.

The negro has been practically eliminated as a

voter, but the decision of the Supreme Court in the Oklahoma case may make necessary the revision of some state constitutions. Enough restrictions remain, however, to make white supremacy reasonably secure for the present. As the aim is one upon which the white South is practically agreed, some other expedients will be devised if those now in use must be discarded. There is absolutely no desire for a wholesale restoration of the negro vote, though, of course, Republican conventions denounce the disfranchising acts and constitutional amendments. If the control of the Southern States should be gained by the Republican party, unlimited negro suffrage would hardly be restored unless such action were forced by the party in the nation at large. In the last extremity the South would suffer loss of representation rather than face the consequences of unrestricted negro suffrage.

Socially the South is in a state of ferment. Old standards are passing, some of them very rapidly, and the younger generation is inclined to smile at some of the attitudes of the old. The "typical Southerner" who flourishes within the pages of F. Hopkinson Smith and Thomas Nelson Page is extremely rare outside of them. Most of the real Southern colonels are dead, and the others are too busy running plantations or cotton mills to spend much time discussing genealogy, making pretty speeches, or talking about their honor. Not so many colonels are made as formerly, and one may travel far before he meets an individual who fits the popular idea of the type. He is likely to meet more men who are cold, hard, and astute, for the New South has developed some perfect specimens of the type whose natural habitat had been supposed to be Ulster or the British Midlands — religious, narrow, stubborn, and very shrewd.

A sense of social responsibility is developing in the South. Kindness has always been shown to the unfortunate and the afflicted, but it has been exhibited toward individuals by individuals. If a Southerner heard of a case of distress in his neighborhood, he was quick to respond. Real neighborliness has always existed, but the idea of responsibility for a class was slow to develop. Such an idea is growing, however. More attention has been given to the condition of jails and almshouses during the last ten years than in the whole preceding century. To be sure, the section is now becoming rich enough to afford the luxury of paupers, but the interest in socialized humanitarian endeavor lies deeper. Perhaps the fact that negroes formed the larger part of the criminal and dependent classes had something to do with the past neglect. The Old Testament doctrine that the criminal should suffer the consequences of his act has had its effect, and the factor of expense has not been forgotten. Some of the States still permit county commissioners to commit the care of the poor to the lowest bidder. On the other hand the poorhouse has been transformed into a "Home for the Aged and Infirm" in some States, and inspections of public institutions by the grand jury are becoming more than merely cursory. State boards of charities are being established, and men have even attacked members of their own political parties on the charge of incompetence, cruelty, or neglect of duty as keepers of prisons or almshouses. Hundreds of towns have their associated charities, and scores have visiting nurses. Where there is only one nurse, she visits negroes as well as whites, but many towns support one or more for negroes as well.

In former days orphans were "bound out," if no relatives would take them, and in that case they might not always be properly treated. At the present time not only States and municipalities support asylums, but religious denominations and

fraternal orders manage many well-conducted institutions. The problem of the juvenile delin-
quent is being recognized, as several States already
have institutions for his care. So far little has been
done for the young negro offender, whose home
training is likely to be most deficient and who
needs firm but kindly discipline; but the consciousness of responsibility for him also is developing.
Increasing prosperity alone cannot account for the
multiplication of these agencies for social betterment. A new social interest and a new attitude of
mind are revealed in these activities.

There are still some communities where social
position is based upon birth and where the old
families still control; but these regions are becoming less numerous. The Old South was never quite
so aristocratic as the North believed, and today the
white South is much more nearly a democracy than
New England. Even in 1860 this was true of some
parts of the South, as compared with some parts of
New England. The rural South was always democratic except in comparatively limited areas, and
it is so everywhere today. In those communities
which have felt the new industrial spirit the question of birth plays little part. Any presentable
young man can go where he chooses. In such

communities the tendency — apparently inevitable in industrial societies — to base social distinctions upon wealth and business success is beginning to show itself. The plutocrats, however, are not yet numerous enough to form a society of their own and must perforce find their associates among their fellow townsmen.

One does not lose social position in the South by engaging in business or by working with his hands. It may easily happen that in the afternoon you may purchase a collar or a pair of shoes from a young man whom you will meet in the evening at the house of the local magnate. The granddaughter of a former governor or justice of the Supreme Court comes home from her typewriter and her brother from the cotton mill or the lumber yard. Social life in a small town — and most Southern towns are small — is simple and unpretentious, although here too the influence of prosperity is beginning to be manifest. Social affairs are more elaborate than they were ten or fifteen years ago, and there is also less casual expression of informal hospitality. The higher prices of food and the increasing difficulties of the servant problem have doubtless put some restraint upon the spirit of hospitality but perhaps more important is the fact that more of the men must keep regular hours of business and that women are developing interests outside the home.

Social affairs are almost entirely in the hands of women. The older men come somewhat unwillingly to receptions in the evening, but the presence of a man at an afternoon tea is unusual. The Southerner of the small towns and cities puts away play with his adolescence. The professional man seldom advertises the fact that he has gone hunting or fishing for a day or a week, as it is thought to be not quite the thing for a lawyer to be away from his office for such a purpose. Golf has gained no foothold except in the larger towns, and even there the existence of the country club is often precarious. Few males except college youths will be seen on the tennis court, if indeed there be one even in a town of five thousand people. Professional men keep long hours, though they might be able to do all their work in half the time they spend in their offices.

The theory of the Old South contemplated different spheres of activity for men and women. The combined influence of St. Paul and Sir Walter Scott is responsible for a part of this theory, though its development was probably inevitable from the

structure of society in the Old South. A woman's
place was the home. As a girl she might live for en-
joyment and spend her time in a round of visits, but
she was expected to give up frivolity of all sorts
when she married. Society in the South was almost entirely the concern of the unmarried. Wom-
en seldom took a prominent part in any organization, and a woman speaking in public was regarded as a great curiosity. Not so many years
ago the missionary society, and perhaps the par-
sonage aid society, were almost the only organizations in which women took a part. In recent years
church and educational organizations have mul-
tiplied, and today there are numerous women's
clubs devoted to many different objects. Southern women are active in civic leagues, associated
charities, and other forms of community endeavor;
they are prominent in various patriotic societies;
and there are many suffrage societies. Where the
laws permit, women are members of school boards;
they often head organizations of teachers composed of both men and women, and at least one
woman has been chosen mayor of a town.

Women have done more than the men to keep
alive in the South the memories of the past. Perhaps because the women of the older generation

14

suffered more than the men, they have been less willing to forget, and their daughters have imbibed some of the same feeling.   The Daughters of the Confederacy have been more bitter than the Sons of Veterans or than the veterans themselves.   The effect of recent events upon their psychology has been interesting.   In the Great War their sons and grandsons were called to go overseas, and the national government was brought closer to them than at any other time for more than forty years.   It is idle to insist that before this there had been any ardent affection in the South for the United States. There had been acceptance of the national situation, perhaps an intellectual acknowledgment that all may have been for the best, but no warm nationalism had been developed before the Great War came.   Loyalty was passive rather than active.

The closing of the chasm has been hailed many times, notably at the time of the Spanish War, but no keen observer has been deceived for a moment. The recent world crisis, however, seems to have swept aside all hindrances.   Perhaps the people, and particularly the women, were unconsciously yearning for a country to love and were ready for a great wave of patriotism to carry them with it. During the week following the declaration of war more national flags were displayed in the South than had been shown in the memory of the oldest resident, for except on public buildings the national flag has not been commonly displayed. At this time houses which had never shown a flag were draped, and merchants were chided because they could not supply the demand.

Quite as a matter of course the president of the Daughters of the Confederacy became president of the Red Cross Auxiliary which was organized at once. Women were eager to receive instruction in folding bandages, and knitting became the order of the day. Women threw themselves with all their energy into various activities. Canteen work was organized if the town was a junction point, and every instalment of "selected men" — for the word "drafted" was rejected almost by common consent — was sent away with some evidence of the thoughtfulness of the women of their home town. Women have been prominent in raising money for the Red Cross and the Y. M. C. A. and have done valiant service in selling War Savings Stamps and Liberty Bonds. There has been some shaking of heads, and some exponents of the sheltered life have criticized this invasion of what had been supposed to be the sphere of men, but the women have gone ahead. Indeed their alacrity has seemed to indicate that they are glad to have an excuse to throw aside the restraints which have hitherto bound them. Women and girls have approached men whom they did not know on the streets to ask for contributions or to urge the purchase of stamps or bonds, and only those who know the South can realize what a departure from traditional standards of feminine conduct such actions indicate. The business woman has been a familiar figure for years, but she was sheltered by the walls of her office or shop. On the street she was held to a certain code and was criticized if she failed to observe it. But here also the old order is changing and giving place to new.

The power of public opinion is very great in the South. While this may be true of rural or semi-rural communities in any part of the land, nowhere else does collective opinion exert such overwhelming force as in the Southern States. Perhaps this phenomenon is a survival from Reconstruction days and after. Since certain attitudes toward the negro, for example, were defended on the ground of the necessity of protecting womanhood, a certain standard must be demanded from women, and every man claimed a sort of prescriptive right to assist in laying down rules for such conduct on her part. For a long time the women of the South, consciously or unconsciously, were subject to these unwritten rules. Today in increasing numbers the women, particularly the younger women, are declaring their independence by their conduct. It has not become a feminist revolt, for many have not thought out the situation and have not recognized the source of their restrictions. The statutes of some of the Southern States, moreover, still contain many of the old common law restrictions upon women's independence of action. More and more women are asserting themselves, however, and are demanding the right to guide themselves. The negro woman has been held up as the reason for denying the vote to the white woman, but this excuse no longer is accepted willingly. Women are inquiring why the vote of the negro women should be any more of a menace than the vote of the negro man, and there seems to be no satisfactory answer. If the women make up their minds and agree, they will gain their ends.

Though women in the South as elsewhere form a majority of the church membership, they have not had equal rights in church administration. During 1918, several denominations granted full laity rights, though the bishops of the Southern Methodist Church referred the action of the General Conference back to the Annual Conferences. This is of course only a temporary delay. An unusually large percentage of the adult population holds membership in one or other of the Protestant denominations. The Roman Catholics are reported as being in a majority in Louisiana, as might be expected owing to French descent, and in Kentucky, Delaware, Maryland, and Texas the proportion is considerable. It is less in Arkansas, Oklahoma, and West Virginia. In Virginia, North Carolina, South Carolina, Georgia, Alabama, Mississippi, and Tennessee, the proportion of Catholics is still smaller, though the latest (1918) official Catholic statistics for the seven States last named show 7 bishops, 415 priests, 635 churches, and 211,-000 Catholics. The principal denominational affiliations of the Southern people, white and black, are with the various Baptist or Methodist bodies, with a strong Presbyterian influence. In eleven of the Southern States the Baptists are by far the largest denomination, though the Methodists lead in two. These two denominations taken together are in a large majority in every State except Delaware, Maryland, and Louisiana. Presbyterians and Episcopalians are well distributed throughout the whole section and have exercised an influence altogether out of proportion to their numbers. Presbyterianism came in with the great Scotch-Irish migration of the eighteenth century, and though many of the blood have gone over to other denominations, the influence of the Shorter Catechism still persists. In the older States attempts were made to establish the Anglican Church in the colonial era, and the governing classes were naturally affiliated with it.

Both these organizations had to give way to the great wave of religious enthusiasm which swept the section early in the nineteenth century. Baptist and Methodist missionaries, many of them unlettered but vigorous and powerful, went into the remotest districts and swept the population into their communions. They preached a narrow, strait-laced, Old Testament religion, but it went deep. They believed in the verbal inspiration of the Bible, and so far as they could they interpreted it literally, laying emphasis upon the future, the rewards of the righteous, and the tortures of the damned. Life upon this earth was regarded as simply a preparation for the life to come. One is sometimes tempted to believe that these spiritual guides deprecated attempts to improve conditions here on earth lest men should grow to think less of a future abode. It is easy to understand why such a doctrine of future reward should have appealed to negroes, and it is perhaps not surprising that the poor upon the frontier likewise found comfort and solace in it. Years ago the social position of the great majority of the Methodists and Baptists was distinctly below that of the Episcopalians and Presbyterians. In recent years many Methodists and Baptists have grown prosperous. Instead of being bare barns, their church edifices are often the most ornate and costly in the town or city. A Methodist or a Baptist can have none of the former feeling of martyrdom now, when in numbers and wealth his denomination is so powerful.[1]

Though the evangelical religious teaching of former days has been modified and softened, it has been softened only and not superseded. The result of this emphasis upon the other world has been to make men look somewhat askance at worldly

[1] Except these five, other church organizations have few members. There are a few Congregationalists, almost entirely the result of post-bellum missions to the negroes. White and negro Lutheran churches are scattered through the Southern States, and in Kentucky and Tennessee the Disciples are important. Here and there other denominations have gained a foothold, but their numbers are insignificant in the South as a whole.

amusement.    The idea so prevalent in other sections that the people of the South are convivial and
mercurial in temperament is erroneous.    It would
be more nearly correct to say that gravity, amounting almost to austerity, is a distinguishing mark of
Southerners.    In any Southern gathering repre-
senting the people as a whole there is little mirth.
There is much more Puritanism in the South today
than remains in New England.    The Sabbath is no
longer observed so strictly as twenty years ago,
perhaps, but only recently has it been considered
proper to receive visits on Sunday or to drive into
the country.    As for Sunday golf or tennis, the
average community would stand horror-struck at
such a spectacle.    Sermons are frequently preached
against dancing, card-playing, and theater-going,
and members have been dismissed from Baptist,
Methodist, and Presbyterian churches for indulging
in these forbidden amusements.

The older generation, however, is losing in the
fight to maintain the old standards of conduct and
belief.    In spite of disapprobation, bridge clubs
flourish and the young people will dance and go to
the theater, though even yet most Southern cities
are known as "poor show towns."    Today men go
to the post office on Sunday, read the Sunday

papers, and ride on Sunday trains. The motor car makes its appearance on Sunday, though it would be interesting to know how many of those riding really feel conscience free, for many who have liberal ideas still have Calvinistic nerves. Young ministers occasionally preach sermons for which they would have been charged with heresy not many years ago and openly read books which would have been considered poisonous then. Men speak of evolution now and show familiarity with authors who were anathema to the older generation.

Lately some of the town and city churches have been developing the social and humanitarian side of religious work, but the greatest number manage to collect only enough money to keep the organization alive. They are like engines which can get up enough steam to turn the wheels slowly and painfully but lack sufficient power to do effective work. In fact, there is strong opposition to any pastor who attempts to influence the decision of the congregation on any social question. Many towns and rural communities have several churches, though their population and wealth may be hardly large enough to support one properly. This condition, however, is not peculiar to the South. Here and there in the country districts a new type of pastor has appeared. He is a good farmer himself, interested in better farming and able to discuss fertilizers and methods with his parishioners. He is not afraid that prosperity will turn his members away from their church duties but considers that improving the economic conditions of the neighborhood is quite as vital a part of his work as ministering to their spiritual needs. Largely because of the work of some of these men the exodus to the towns has slackened in some neighborhoods and contributions to the work of the church have been greatly increased.

This movement from country to town has become a serious matter in some localities. The social level of neighborhoods once attractive because of the presence of families of intelligence and character has fallen. The land of the families which have moved to towns has been turned over to tenants, either whites of a lower status or negroes, the standards of the community have suffered in consequence, and the atmosphere of some of these communities has become depressing. Such conditions, however, are not peculiar to the South but have been observed in central New York and in New England. Better roads, the motor car, and improvement in communications have helped to check this cityward movement, and, on the whole, the educational, economic, and social standards of the country districts generally are higher than they were ten years ago.

Generally speaking, the South is a law-abiding section. This is true even when the negroes are included, and as the prohibitory laws are enforced more strictly, it is becoming increasingly true. The chain gang which was so common years ago has been discontinued in hundreds of counties, chiefly for lack of convicts, though partly for humanitarian reasons. The offenses of the negro were, for the most part, petty larceny, gambling, and offenses against public order. Affrays are certainly less frequent since the spread of prohibition, and larceny seems to be decreasing, though statistics of crime are few and unreliable. The gambling is usually nothing more than "craps," or "African billiards" as they call it now. Among the whites, offenses against property are few. In many rural counties a white man is seldom charged with theft, fraud, or forgery. A white man is occasionally arraigned for "disposing of mortgaged property," or for malicious mischief, including the destruction of property.

The homicide rate, however, is high. Generally

the figures given include the negro, and he is somewhat more homicidal than the white, but the white
rate is among the highest in the world. Blood
feuds actually exist in the Southern Appalachians,
though perhaps their number is not so large as is
commonly believed. The moonshiner's antipathy
to revenue officers leads him to use firearms upon
occasion, but homicide occurs also in intelligent
communities where the general tone is high. Individuals of excellent standing in business or professional life sometimes shoot to kill their fellows
and in the past have usually escaped the extreme
penalty and often have avoided punishment altogether. It would seem that life is held rather
cheaply in many Southern communities.

Until recently much of the South has remained a
frontier, as some of it is to this day, and in frontier
communities men are accustomed to take the law
into their own hands and are reluctant to depend
upon inadequate or ineffective police protection.
Despising physical cowardice, the individual prides
himself upon his ability to maintain his rights and
to protect his honor without calling for assistance.
Frontiersmen are quick to resent an affront, and
when their veracity is impugned they fight. The
word "lie" is not considered a polite mode of

expressing dissent. All over the South, in every class of society, one finds this sensitiveness to an accusation of lack of veracity. Such a theory of life dies hard. The presence of a less advanced race is perhaps not conducive to self-control. The dominant race, determined to maintain its position of superiority, is likely to resent a real or fancied affront to its dignity. A warped sense of honor, a sort of belated theory of chivalry, is responsible for some acts of violence. A seducer is likely to be called to account and the slayer, by invoking the "unwritten law," has usually been acquitted. Such a case lends itself to the display of flamboyant oratory, and the plea of "protecting the home" has set many murderers free. Perhaps the South is becoming less susceptible to oratory; at all events this plea now sometimes fails to win a jury. Defendants are occasionally convicted, though the verdicts are usually rendered for manslaughter and not for murder.

Public sentiment is not yet ready, however, to declare every intentional homicide murder. Some point to the low rate of white illegitimacy as a justification of the deterring force of the "unwritten law," not realizing that such a defense is really a reflection upon womanhood. Others allow

their detestation of physical cowardice to blind
them to the danger of allowing men to take the law
into their own hands.   The individualism of the
imperfectly socialized Southerner does not yet permit him to think of the law as a majestic, imper-
sonal force towering high above the individual.   It
is true that the Southerner is law-abiding on the
whole, but he usually obeys the laws because they
represent his ethical concepts and not because of
devotion to the abstract idea of law.

There is danger, however, in the attempt to
state dogmatically what the Southerner thinks or
believes.   There is much diversity of opinion
among the younger Southerners, for many questions are in a state of flux, and there is as yet no
point of crystallization.   There is no leader either
in politics or in journalism who may be said to
utter the voice of the South.   In the earlier part
of this period Henry Watterson, of the Louisville
*Courier-Journal*, spoke almost with authority.   The
untimely death of Henry W. Grady, editor of the
Atlanta *Constitution*, deprived the South of a
spokesman and he has had no successor.   There
is no newspaper which has any considerable influence outside the State in which it is published, and
few have a circulation throughout even their entire

State.   There are several newspapers which are
edited with considerable ability, on the political
side at least, but none has a circulation sufficiently
large to make it a real power.   All are more or less
parochial.   The country papers, which are frankly
and necessarily local, exercise more influence than
the papers of the cities, though the circulation of
the latter is increasing.

The Southerner is reading more than he once did.
Some of the national weeklies have a considerable
circulation in the South, and the national magazines are read in increasing numbers.   Good book-
stores are not common, for the people generally
have not learned to buy many books since they have
been able to afford them.   The women's clubs,
however, interest their members in the "best-sell-
ers" and pass these books from one to another.
Some members may always be depended upon to
purchase serious books as their contribution to the
club.   The number of public libraries in the South
is considerable, and the educational administration of several of the States is striving to put a
well-selected library into every public school.[1]

[1] North Carolina has established over five thousand of these school
libraries.   The State pays one-third of the cost, the county one-third,
and the patrons of the school the remainder.   Additional volumes are
furnished by the same plan.

The Southerner is not only reading more books, but he is also writing more. A man or woman who has written a book is no longer a curiosity. In the closing decade or two of the nineteenth century the work of a group of Southern writers led a distinguished critic to rank them as the most significant force in American letters. Such a high valuation of the writers of the present day could hardly be made, but there is a much larger number than formerly whose work is acceptable. Members of college faculties, and others, produce annually numerous books of solid worth in science, history, biography, economics, and sociology. Volumes of recollections and reminiscences interesting to the student of the past appear, and much local and state history has been rescued from oblivion. Some theological books are written, but there is little published on national questions. The output of verse is small, and few essays are published. As few Southerners are extensive travelers, there are necessarily few books of travel and description. Though most of the people live in a rural or semi-rural environment, very little is printed dealing with nature. There are many writers of fiction, though few can be called artists.

The New South is full of contradictions and

15

paradoxes. It is living generations of social and economic changes in decades, and naturally all the people do not keep an even pace. One may find culture that would grace a court alongside incredible ignorance; distinguished courtesy and sheer brutality; kindness and consideration of the rights and feelings of others together with cruelty almost unbelievable. In some sections are to be found machines belonging to the most advanced stage of industry, while nearby are in operation economic processes of the rudest and most primitive sort. One who knows the South must feel, however, that its most striking characteristic is hopefulness. The dull apathy of a generation ago is rapidly disappearing, and the South lifts up its eyes toward the future.

# THE REPUDIATION OF STATE DEBTS

THE debt of Mississippi was small and that of Texas was not excessive, and neither made any attempt to repudiate the obligations. The $4,000,000 issued in Florida for state aid to railroads was large for the small population and the scanty resources of that State, but this issue was declared unconstitutional by the Supreme Court of Florida. The Reconstruction debt of Alabama was large, about $20,000,000, besides accrued interest which the State could not pay. In 1873, the carpet-bag government attempted to fund these bonds at twenty-five cents on the dollar. The Funding Act of 1876 repudiated $4,700,000 outright, reduced the bonds loaned to one railroad from $5,300,000 to $1,000,000, gave land in payment of $2,000,000 more, scaled other bonds one-half, and funded still others at par excluding interest. About $13,000,000 in all was repudiated and the State was left with a debt of less than $10,000,000.[1]

During 1868 and 1869 bond issues to the amount of nearly $28,000,000 were authorized in North Carolina, but not all of this amount was issued. From the $13,313,000 which was outstanding at the end of the carpetbag régime, the State had received little or no benefit. Interest was not paid upon this sum or upon

[1] W. A. Scott, *The Repudiation of State Debts*, p. 63, but see also W. L. Fleming, *Civil War and Reconstruction in Alabama*, p. 580 ff.

the previous issues, and the total debt increased rapidly. Unsuccessful attempts to compromise with the creditors were made in 1874 and 1875, but not until 1879 was the matter settled. The Reconstruction bonds were repudiated outright, and the legitimate debt of the State was funded at from fifteen to forty cents on the dollar. No provision was made for the unpaid interest. This compromise did not include the pre-war bonds issued to aid the North Carolina Railroad. This corporation was a going concern, and as the result of a suit the stock had been sequestrated. A compromise with the holders of these bonds was made at eighty per cent of par and interest. As a result of this wholesale repudiation the debt of the State was so reduced that it could be carried. In all over $22,000,000 besides other millions of accrued interest were repudiated.[1]

Not all of the creditors of the State accepted the compromise at once, but the offer was left open and, as the years went on and the State showed no signs of a change of intention, the bondholders gradually recognized the inevitable. In 1893, nearly fifteen years after this offer had been made, more than $1,000,000 of the old bonds were still outstanding. In 1901, a New York firm presented to the State of South Dakota ten of the class which had been made convertible at twenty-five cents on the dollar. That State brought suit in the Supreme Court of the United States and collected the amount sued for.[2] No progress has been made in collecting the special tax bonds issued during Reconstruction though some New York bond houses hope against hope, and the

[1] J. G. de R. Hamilton, *Reconstruction in North Carolina*, pp. 448–449, 659–661.

[2] South Dakota *v.* North Carolina, 192 U. S. Rep., p. 286.

Council of the Corporation of Foreign Bondholders in its annual reports plaintively regrets the perversity of this and other Southern States.

South Carolina presented such a carnival of incompetence and corruption that the total amount of bonds issued has never been accurately determined. Apparently there was a valid debt of about $6,666,000 in 1868, which was increased to about $29,000,000 within three years. The carpetbag Legislature of 1873 repudiated $6,000,000 of this debt, and attempted to compromise the remainder at fifty per cent, but the State could not carry even this reduced amount. Judicial decisions destroyed the validity of some millions more, and finally the debt, reduced to something more than $7,000,000, was funded. The debt of Georgia was increased directly and by indorsement of railroad bonds. The Legislature of 1872 declared $8,500,000 void and in 1875 repudiated about $600,000 more.

Louisiana suffered most from excessive taxation. At the beginning of the carpetbag period the debt was about $11,000,000, but railroad and levee bonds were issued rapidly. Though a constitutional amendment in 1870 forbade the State to contract debts in excess of $25,000,000, the Legislature went steadily on until in 1872 the debt was variously estimated at from $41,000,-000 to $48,000,000. In 1874, when W. P. Kellogg was Governor, the State began to fund valid obligations at sixty cents on the dollar. By action of the courts the debt was reduced to about $12,000,000 bearing interest at seven per cent. The State could not pay the interest on this sum, and the constitutional convention of 1879 made drastic reductions in the interest rate. Both New York and New Hampshire, acting ostensibly for themselves but really in behalf of their citizens, brought suit, but the Supreme Court threw out the cases on the ground that the actions were attempts to evade the constitutional provision forbidding a citizen to bring an action against a State. The bondholders still refused to accept the reduction, and the Supreme Court in 1883 described the ordinance as a violation of the contract of 1874 but a violation without a remedy. Meanwhile the Legislature, after consultation with the bondholders, had agreed to a slight increase in the rate of interest; and in 1884, this compromise was ratified by an amendment to the constitution.

The debt of Arkansas was not so difficult to settle. The issue of about $7,500,000 for railroads and levees during Reconstruction was declared unconstitutional in 1877–78, and the so-called Holford bonds, issued in aid of banks, were repudiated by the constitutional convention of 1884. The total amount repudiated and declared void by the courts was nearly $13,000,000. Tennessee also struggled with a debt which it was unwilling and perhaps unable to pay. The amount, which in 1861 was about $21,000,000, incurred principally in aid of railroads and turnpikes, was largely increased under Republican rule, and most of the money received for the bonds was stolen or wasted. No interest had been paid during the War, and the accrued interest was funded in 1865, 1869, and 1873. The debt was somewhat reduced by permitting the railroads to pay their debt in state bonds which they purchased cheaply on the market. Other defaulting railroads were sold, but the State still could not meet the interest. Many discussions with the creditors were held, but the people had the idea that much of the debt was fraudulent and they consequently voted down proposals which they thought too liberal to the creditors. The question temporarily split the Democratic party, but after much discussion a long act was passed in 1883 which finally settled the matter. A part of the debt, with interest, was funded at 76 to 80 cents on the dollar. The major part was funded at 50 cents on the dollar with interest thereafter at three per cent.

The financial difficulties of Virginia excited more interest than did those of any other commonwealth, for this State had the largest pre-war debt. Its $33,000,000 with accrued interest had amounted to about $45,000,-000 in 1870. In 1871 the question of settlement was taken up; one-third of the debt was assigned to West Virginia, and the remainder was funded into new bonds bearing interest at five and six per cent. The coupons were made receivable for taxes and other debts due the State. The amount recognized was beyond the ability of the State to pay, and many members of both parties felt that some compromise must be made. So many of the coupons were paid in for taxes that money to keep the Government going was found with difficulty. Various attacks on the privilege were made, but these "coupon killers" were usually declared unconstitutional by the Supreme Court of the United States. Meanwhile the contest had split the State. Some were in favor of paying the whole debt according to the agreement of 1871; others wished to reduce the interest rate; while the radicals wished to repudiate part of the debt and reduce the rate of interest upon the remainder. The last named faction, under the leadership of H. H. Riddleberger, organized a political party known as the Readjusters and in 1879 captured the Legislature. Riddleberger then introduced a bill which scaled down the debt to less than $20,000,-000, but it was vetoed by the Governor. Two years later the new party captured both Governorship and Legislature and sent General William Mahone to the United States Senate, where he usually voted with the Republican party.

The Legislature repassed the Riddleberger bill, which the creditors refused to accept, and an ingenious "coupon killer." Similar acts were passed in 1886 and 1887. The United States Supreme Court, before which these acts were brought, pronounced them unconstitutional in that they impaired the obligation of contracts, but the Court also stated that there was no way in which the State could be coerced. Meanwhile the credit of the State was nonexistent, and all business suffered. In 1890 a commission reported in favor of compromising the debt on the lines of the Riddleberger Act and, in 1892, $19,000,000 in new bonds were exchanged for about $28,000,000 of the older issue. Interest was to be 2 per cent for ten years and then 3 per cent for ninety more.

West Virginia steadfastly refused to recognize the share of the debt assigned to her on the ground that the principal part had been incurred for internal improvements in Virginia proper, and that one-third was an excessive proportion. The matter dragged along until the Supreme Court of the United States decided in March, 1911, that the equitable proportion due by West Virginia was 23.5 per cent instead of one-third. West Virginia, however, made no move to carry out the decision, and in 1914 Virginia asked the Court to proceed to a final decree. A special master was appointed to take testimony, and on June 14, 1915, the Supreme Court announced that the net share of West Virginia was $12,393,929 plus $8,178,000 interest. The State, by a compromise with Virginia in 1919, assumed a debt amounting to $14,500,000.

# BIBLIOGRAPHICAL NOTE

MANY of the references for the period of Reconstruction are also valuable for the subject of this volume, as it is impossible to understand the South today without understanding the period which preceded it. Much enlightening material is to be found in W. L. Fleming's *Documentary History of Reconstruction* (2 vols., 1906–07) and in the series of monographs on Reconstruction published by the students of Professor W. A. Dunning of Columbia University, among which may be mentioned J. W. Garner's *Reconstruction in Mississippi* (1901); W. L. Fleming's *Civil War and Reconstruction in Alabama* (1905); J. G. de R. Hamilton's *Reconstruction in North Carolina* (1914); C. M. Thompson's *Reconstruction in Georgia, Economic, Social, Political, 1865–1872* (1915).

## GENERAL WORKS

Some of the older books are interesting from the historical standpoint, but conditions in the South have changed so rapidly that these works give little help in understanding the present. Among the most interesting are A. W. Tourgée's *Appeal to Caesar* (1884), based upon the belief that the South would soon be

overwhelmingly black.    Alexander K. McClure, in
*The South; its Industrial, Financial and Political Condi-
tion* (1886), was one of the first to take a hopeful view
of the economic development of the Southern States.
W. D. Kelley's *The Old South and the New* (1887) contains the observations of a shrewd Pennsylvania politician who was intensely interested in the economic
development of the United States.    Walter H. Page's
*The Rebuilding of Old Commonwealths* (1902) is a keen
analysis of the factors which have hindered progress
in the South.

No recent work fully covers this period.    Most
books deal chiefly with individual phases of the question.    Some valuable material may be found in the
series *The South in the Building of the Nation*, 13 vols.,
(1909–13) but not all of this information is trustworthy.
The *Library of Southern Literature* (16 vols., 1907–
1913), edited by E. A. Alderman and Joel Chandler
Harris, contains selections from Southern authors and
biographical notes.    Albert Bushnell Hart's *The Southern South* (1910) is the result of more study and in-
vestigation than any other Northerner has given to
the sociology of the South, but the author's prejudices
interfere with the value of his conclusions.    The late
Edgar Gardner Murphy in *Problems of the Present
South* (1904) discusses with wisdom and sanity many
Southern questions which are still undecided.    A
series of valuable though unequal papers is *The New
South* in the *Annals of the American Academy of Political and Social Science*, vol. 35 (1910).    Another co-
operative work which contains material of value is
*Studies in Southern History and Politics*, edited by J.
W. Garner (1914).    *Why the Solid South*, edited by H.

A. Herbert (1890), should also be consulted. A bitter arraignment of the South as a whole is H. E. Tremain's *Sectionalism Unmasked* (1907). The best book on the Appalachian South is Horace Kephart's *Our Southern Highlanders* (1913). William Garrott Brown's *The Lower South in American History* (1902) contains some interesting matter.

## ECONOMIC DEVELOPMENT

There are several excellent works on cotton and the cotton trade, chief among which are M. B. Hammond's *The Cotton Industry* (1897) and C. W. Burkett and C. H. Poe's *Cotton, its Cultivation, Marketing, Manufacture, and the Problems of the Cotton World* (1906). D. A. Tompkins, in *Cotton and Cotton Oil* (1901), gives valuable material but is rather discursive. J. A. B. Scherer, in *Cotton as a World Power* (1916), attempts to show the influence of cotton upon history. Holland Thompson in *From the Cotton Field to the Cotton Mill* (1906) deals with the economic and social changes arising from the development of manufacturing in an agricultural society. With this may be mentioned A. Kohn's *The Cotton Mills of South Carolina* (1907). M. T. Copeland's *The Cotton Manufacturing Industry of the United States* (1912) has some interesting chapters on the South. T. M. Young, an English labor leader, in *The American Cotton Industry* (1903), brings a fresh point of view. The files of the *Manufacturer's Record* (Baltimore) are indispensable to a student of the economic progress of the South.

## THE NEGRO QUESTION

The number of books, pamphlets, and special articles upon this subject, written by Northerners, Southerners, negroes, and even foreigners, is enormous. These publications range from displays of hysterical emotionalism to statistical studies, but no one book can treat fully all phases of so complex a question. Bibliographies have been prepared by W. E. B. Du Bois, A. P. C. Griffin, and others. W. L. Fleming has appended a useful list of titles to *Reconstruction of the Seceded States* (1905).

F. L. Hoffman, a professional statistician of German birth, in *Race Traits and Tendencies of the American Negro* (1896), has collected much valuable material but all his conclusions cannot be accepted without question. Special *Bulletins* on the negro are published by the United States Census Bureau, of which the issues for 1904 and 1915 should especially be consulted. Some of the *Publications* of Atlanta University contain valuable studies of special localities or occupations.

Several negroes have written histories of their race. George W. Williams's *History of the Negro Race in America from 1619 to 1880*, 2 vols. (1883), is old but contains material of value. William H. Thomas, in *The American Negro* (1901), is pessimistic as to the future because of the moral delinquencies of his people. Booker T. Washington's *The Story of the Negro, the Rise of the Race from Slavery* (1909), on the other hand, emphasizes achievements rather than deficiencies and is optimistic in tone. Of this writer's several other books, the *Future of the American Negro* (1899) is the most valuable. Kelly Miller has written *Race Adjustment*

(1908) and *An Appeal to Conscience* (1918), besides
many articles and monographs all marked by excellent
temper.   On the other hand, W. E. B. Du Bois, in
*The Souls of Black Folk* (1903) and in his other writ-
ings, voices the bitterness of one to whom the color line
has proved an "intolerable indignity."

Ray Stannard Baker in *Following the Color Line*
(1908) gives the observations of a trained metropolitan
journalist and is eminently sane in treatment.   William Archer, the English author and journalist ex-
presses a European point of view in *Through Afro-
America* (1910).   Carl Kelsey's *The Negro Farmer*
(1903) is a careful study of agricultural conditions in
eastern Virginia.   A collection of valuable though unequal papers is contained in the *Annals of the American Academy of Political and Social Science* under *The
Negro's Progress in Fifty Years*, No. 138 (1913) and
*America's Race Problem* (1901).

One of the first Southerners to attack the new problem was A. G. Haygood, later a Bishop of the Methodist Episcopal Church, South, who published *Our
Brother in Black, His Freedom and His Future* (1881).
P. A. Bruce, in *The Plantation Negro as a Freeman*
(1888), has done an excellent piece of work.   Thomas
Nelson Page, in *The Negro, The Southerner's Problem*
(1904), holds that no good can come through outside
interference.   William B. Smith's *The Color Line*
(1905) takes the position that the negro is fundamentally different from the white.   Alfred Holt Stone, in
*Studies in the American Race Problem* (1908), has given
a record of his experiences and reflections as a cotton
planter in the delta region of Mississippi, while Pa-
tience Pennington (*pseud.*) in *A Woman Rice-Planter*

(1913) gives in the form of a diary a naïve but fascinating account of life in the lowlands of South Carolina. Edgar Gardner Murphy, whose *Problems of the Present South* has already been mentioned, discusses in *The Basis of Ascendancy* (1909) the proper relations of black and white. The title of Gilbert T. Stephenson's *Race Distinctions in American Law* (1910) is self-explanatory.

## EDUCATION

No complete history of education in the South has been written. The United States Bureau of Education published years ago several monographs upon the separate States. Edgar W. Knight has written an excellent history of *Public School Education in North Carolina* (1916). Carter G. Woodson, *The Education of the Negro Prior to 1861* (1915), E. A. Alderman's *J. L. M. Curry, a Biography* (1911), and R. D. W. Connor and C. W. Poe's *Life and Speeches of Charles Brantley Aycock* (1912) are illuminating. J. L. M. Curry's *A Brief Sketch of George Peabody and a History of the Peabody Education Fund through Thirty Years* (1898) gives an excellent idea of the situation after Reconstruction. *The General Education Board; an Account of its Activities, 1902–1914* (1915) contains interesting facts on the educational situation of today. The reports of the state Departments of Education, of the United States Bureau of Education, of the Conference for Education in the South, and of the Peabody, Slater, and Jeanes Funds should be consulted. The two volumes on *Negro Education*, United States Bureau of Education Bulle-

tins Nos. 38 and 39 (1916) are invaluable. There are
also histories of some of the state universities and of
the church and private schools.

## FICTION

Some of the best historical material on the changing
South is in the form of fiction. A number of gifted
writers have pictured limited fields with skill and
truth. Mary Noailles Murfree (*pseud.*, Charles Eg-
bert Craddock) has written of the mountain people of
Tennessee, while John Fox, Jr. has done the same for
Kentucky and the Virginia and West Virginia mountains. George W. Cable and Grace King have de-
picted Louisiana in the early part of this period, while
rural life in Georgia has been well described in the
stories of Joel Chandler Harris, better known from his
Uncle Remus books. In *The Voice of the People* (1900)
Ellen Glasgow has produced, in the form of fiction, an
important historical document on the rise of the common man. In *The Southerner* (1909) Nicholas Worth
(understood to be the pseudonym of a distinguished
editor and diplomat) has made a careful study of conditions in North Carolina between 1875 and 1895, while
Thomas Dixon in *The Leopard's Spots* (1902) has crude-
ly but powerfully drawn a picture of the campaign
for negro disfranchisement in that State.

In his *Old Judge Priest* stories, Irvin S. Cobb has
described the rural towns of Kentucky; and Corra
Harris from personal experience has given striking
pictures of the rural South principally in relation to
religion. The short stories of Harris Dickson portray
the negro of the Mississippi towns. The stories of

16

Thomas Nelson Page and of Ruth McEnery Stuart
should also be mentioned.   Owen Wister has drawn a
striking picture of Charleston in *Lady Baltimore*
(1906), while Henry Sydnor Harrison in *Queed* (1911)
and his later stories has done something similar for
Richmond.

# INDEX

Agricultural Wheel, 34

Agriculture, farmers' revolt, 31 *et seq.*; farmer and the land, 60 *et seq.*; county demonstrators, 75–77, 184; Farm Loan Act, 84; influence on labor, 116; economic future of South in, 198–99

Alabama, Conservative party in, 12; Kolb in, 37–38; Populist party, 42; suffrage amendments, 54–55; boys' corn club, 79; cotton mills, 97; iron industry, 101; mines, 102; bituminous coal, 102; school fund, 158 (note); Catholics in, 214; repudiation of debt, 227

American Tobacco Company, 103

Archer, William, *Through Afro-America*, quoted, 141

Arkansas, hillmen of, 6; Agricultural Wheel in, 34; election (1896), 44; lumbering, 100; mixed schools, 161; industrialism, 193; migration to, 194; woman suffrage, 202; Catholics in, 214; repudiation of debt, 230–31

Atlanta (Ga.), Cotton Exposition (1881), 89

Aycock, C. B., Governor of North Carolina, 57

Badeau, General Adam, and expression "New South," 7

Baptist Church, 214, 215–16

Bayard, T. F., of Delaware, 28

Birmingham (Ala.), steel center, 101–02

Blair Bill, 27

Blease, C. L., of South Carolina, 122, 150

Boys 'and girls' clubs, 76, 78–81

Brothers of Freedom, 34

Bryan, W. J., presidential nomination, 44

Buck, S. J., *The Agrarian Crusade*, cited, 25 (note), 44 (note)

Butler, Marion, of North Carolina, 43

Butler, M. C., of South Carolina, 13, 41

Calhoun, J. C., agricultural college founded on plantation of, 42

Carlisle, J. G., of Kentucky, 29

Carnegie Foundation and college standards, 189

Carolinas, differing economic conditions, 6; Scotch-Irish in, 6; *see also* North Carolina, South Carolina

Carpetbaggers' rule overthrown, 9, 12

Catholic Church, 214

Charleston (S. C.), party management in, 39; Tillman and, 40

Child labor, state restrictions, 97, 118; in cotton mills, 109, 114–15, 117; Federal Child Labor Act, 118